DATE DUE			

5608

B
GOD

Coil, Suzanne M.

Robert Hutchings
Goddard : pioneer of
rocketry and space
flight.

ROBERT HUTCHINGS GODDARD

Also by Suzanne M. Coil

Florida
George Washington Carver
Poisonous Plants
The Poor in America

Makers of Modern Science

ROBERT HUTCHINGS GODDARD
Pioneer of Rocketry and Space Flight

Suzanne M. Coil

Facts On File
New York • Oxford

ROBERT HUTCHINGS GODDARD: Pioneer of Rocketry and Space Flight

Facts On File, Inc.
460 Park Avenue South
New York NY 10016
USA

Facts On File Limited
c/o Roundhouse Publishing Ltd.
P. O. Box 140
Oxford OX2 7SF
United Kingdom

Library of Congress Cataloging-in-Publication Data
Coil, Suzanne M.
  Robert Hutchings Goddard : pioneer of rocketry and space flight / Suzanne M. Coil.
     p. cm. — (Makers of modern science)
  Includes bibliographical references and index.
  Summary: Discusses the life and achievements of a pioneer in the fields of rocketry and space flight.
  ISBN 0-8160-2591-6 (alk. paper)
  1. Goddard, Robert Hutchings, 1882–1945—Juvenile literature.
2. Rocketry—United States—Biography—Juvenile literature.
3. Astronautics—United States—Biography—Juvenile literature.
[1. Goddard, Robert Hutchings, 1882–1945. 2. Scientists.
3. Rocketry.]   I. Title.   II. Series.
  TL781.85.G6C65   1992
  629.4'092—dc20
  [B]   91-47503

A British CIP catalogue record for this book is available from the British Library.

Facts On File books are available at special discounts when purchased in bulk quantities for businesses, associations, institutions or sales promotions. Please call our Special Sales Department in New York at 212/683-2244 (dial 800/322-8755 except in NY, AK or HI) or in Oxford at 865/728399.

Text design by Ron Monteleone
Jacket design by Catherine Hyman
Composition by Facts On File, Inc.
Manufactured by R. R. Donnelley & Sons
Printed in the United States of America

10 9 8 7 6 5 4 3 2 1

This book is printed on acid-free paper.

For my favorite men of science
René Matthias Coil,
Christopher-Keith Lenox,
and
Charles K. Wolf

"Often a science in its infancy, because it is unable to distinguish between path and barrier, falsely judges many things to be possible and others to be impossible; and an individual, setting out on his career, is often prone to consider that he knows what is open to him and what is closed. But, just as in the sciences we have learned that we are too ignorant safely to pronounce anything impossible, so for the individual . . . we can hardly say with certainty that anything is necessarily within or beyond his grasp. Each must remember that no one can predict to what heights of wealth, fame or usefulness he may rise until he has honestly endeavored, and he should derive courage from the fact that all sciences have been, at some time, in the same condition as he, and that it has often proved true that the dream of yesterday is the hope of today and the reality of tomorrow."

From *On Taking Things for Granted*
Robert Hutchings Goddard's
Graduation Oration
South High School
Worcester, Massachusetts
June 24, 1904

CONTENTS

Acknowledgments viii

1. Impossible Dreams 1
2. A Different Boy 11
3. Newton's Law 24
4. Moon Man 39
5. Lox and Love 50
6. Two-and-a-Half Seconds to History 60
7. Lucky Lindy 74
8. The Desert 82
9. Countdown to Success 92
10. War 103
11. Epilogue 115

Milestones in the Rocket Experiments of
  Robert H. Goddard 121
Glossary 123
Further Reading 126
Index 129

ACKNOWLEDGMENTS

I wish to thank Brigadier General Homer A. Boushey, U.S.A.F. (Ret.); Ralph W. Gilbert; Robert W. Lord; Mrs. Barbara Peck; and Richard C. Pullinger, A.I.A. for their kindness and generosity in sharing their personal memories of Dr. Goddard. I am also grateful for the information supplied by Raymond A. Broms Jr., president of the Chicago Air Mail Society; Daniel R. Cedrone; Tom A. Farrell; Frank H. Winter, curator of Rocketry at the National Air and Space Museum, Smithsonian Institution; and employees of NASA's Goddard Space Flight Center in Greenbelt, Maryland. Above all, I wish to thank Dorothy E. Mosakowski, coordinator of Archives and Special Collections at the Robert Hutchings Goddard Library, Clark University, Worcester, Massachusetts, for her gracious assistance.

—S. M. C.
Covington, Louisiana
1992

1

IMPOSSIBLE DREAMS

"It shall be done, said I, and away I set out for heaven . . . in a little time the Earth was invisible, and the Moon appeared very small; and now, leaving the Sun on my right hand, I flew among the stars."

—Lucian of Samosata

Since the dawn of history, people have dreamed of escaping the bonds of Earth to explore the heavens beyond. In the second century A.D., a Greek writer named Lucian of Samosata wrote what are probably the first works of fiction describing space travel. In his *Vera Historia (True History)*, Lucian described a trip to the moon in a sailing ship. In a second book, *Icaro-Menippus*, Lucian's hero used the wings of birds to fly to the moon.

In the centuries that followed, the idea of space travel continued to engage the human imagination. While fantastic schemes to send people journeying beyond the Earth appeared with regularity from the pens of fiction writers, astronomers and physicists studied the universe and refined their theories about the laws governing its operation. During the Industrial Revolution of the 19th century, great advances in technology demonstrated how scientific principles could be applied in practical ways and convinced people that anything humans set their minds to could be accomplished. By the beginning of the 20th century, the idea of space travel no longer seemed to be an entirely impossible notion, and a handful of scientists turned their attention to the practical problems involved in exploring worlds beyond our own.

Robert Hutchings Goddard (1882–1945). (Goddard Collection/Clark University)

Finally, on July 30, 1969, the dream of centuries became a reality. While millions of people around the world gathered in front of television sets to watch in awe, astronauts Neil A. Armstrong and Edwin E. Aldrin Jr. stepped from their Apollo spacecraft to become the first human beings ever to set foot on the moon.

Among the cheering crowds at the Cape Canaveral launching site were hundreds of scientists and technicians. Although they had worked long and hard to make this dramatic achievement possible, they knew that the success of the mission was based on the knowledge gained through lonely experimentation many years before by a dedicated man who was given little support during his lifetime. But the man who pioneered humankind's most daring adventure was not present. Robert Hutchings Goddard, America's foremost space researcher, had died nearly 24 years before. Now, many years after his death, space scientists honor Robert Hutchings Goddard as the "Father of Modern Rocketry"—the man whose accomplishments paved the way for the trip to the moon, the space shuttle, the exploration of the solar system, and all other space missions.

When Robert Hutchings Goddard was born on October 5, 1882, in Worcester, Massachusetts, space travel was still a distant dream. Newspapers that year were filled with stories of exciting technological events that were taking place on planet Earth. The Brooklyn Bridge was under construction in New York City, plans were being laid to erect the Statue of Liberty in New York harbor, and the French were attempting to dig a canal across the Isthmus of Panama. In Appleton, Wisconsin, the great inventor Thomas Alva Edison designed the first operating hydroelectric plant—an invention that was to transform life in America. And in England, an engineer named Hiram S. Maxim patented a recoil-operated machine gun that was to revolutionize warfare.

It was an exciting time for the young Goddard family as well. When Robert was less than a year old, a Boston acquaintance offered his father a half interest in a machine knife shop. The Goddards looked forward to life in the city, and before long, Bob and his parents, Nahum Danford Goddard and Fannie Hoyt Goddard, were installed in their new home at 63 Forest Street in Boston.

As a young child, Bob Goddard was filled with curiosity about the world around him. His bright, intelligent eyes noticed everything, and his restless mind was filled with questions. He was interested in animals, insects, and plants. He was equally fascinated by tools and mechanisms. "I imagine an innate interest in mechanical things was inherited from a number of ancestors who were machinists," he later wrote. Heredity may have played a role, but it is certain that Bob's own intelligence and imagination were hard at work. He liked to take things apart to see how they functioned, and no clock or mechanical device in the Goddard household escaped his investigations. With a burning need to know and to find out things for himself, Bob decided to conduct experiments of his own.

On a visit to his uncle's workshop, five-year-old Bob witnessed something amazing—a battery that produced electricity. At home, he found that he, too, could produce electric sparks—by scuffing his feet on a carpet. He reasoned that if he rubbed zinc from a battery on the soles of his shoes and then scuffed them along the gravel walk next to the house, he might produce a spark powerful enough to lift him off the Earth. One day, he decided to test his theory. After rubbing zinc on his shoes and scuffing them vigorously on the gravel walk, he climbed a low fence and jumped. He repeated the experiment several times, scuffing over longer distances, and jumping again and again—convinced that the longer he scuffed, the higher he could jump. Alarmed by the sight of Bob leaping off the fence, Fannie Goddard asked her son what he was doing. When Bob explained, his mother warned him to be careful. What would happen, she asked, if his experiment was successful and he sailed away without being able to come back? It was a risk young Bob was unwilling to take. Reluctantly, he put the zinc rod away and abandoned his experiment.

Bob was an only child who enjoyed a warm, close relationship with his parents. Impressed by his restless intelligence, Nahum and Fannie Goddard encouraged their son's interest in science by allowing him to conduct sometimes dubious experiments and by supplying him with useful tools, including a microscope, a telescope, and a subscription to *Scientific American*. Nor did they object when Bob sent away to scientific mail-order firms for things that would help him carry out his ideas for a perpetual motion machine, experiments with kites, and a variety of other projects.

"My father and I were great pals," Bob later wrote, describing a trip to Worcester one summer, "and spent the time tramping through the country." It was his first trip away from the narrow confines of the Goddards' Boston home. The mysterious beauty of the woods and ponds on the outskirts of the town impressed Bob deeply, and the wildlife he and his father encountered aroused his interest. It was during this trip that Bob focused his attention on frogs.

Robert H. Goddard, shown sitting on the steps of Maple Hill, in Worcester, Massachusetts, was about seven years old when this picture was taken. With him are (l. to r.) his mother, Fannie Hoyt Goddard; his grandmother, Mary Upham Goddard; his great-grandmother, Elvira Goddard Ward; and his father, Nahum D. Goddard. (Goddard Collection/Clark University)

Fascinated by their ability to leap great heights and distances in relation to their body size, Bob spent the following winter drawing elaborate plans for a "frog hatchery" so that he could raise frogs and study them more closely. He carefully jotted down his plans and ideas in a notebook, a habit that he was to continue throughout his life. He pursued his interest in raising frogs for several years, although he later confessed that planning waterwheels and engines for the hatchery were the most fascinating part of the project.

Bob did well at school and was popular with his classmates, but frequent colds and recurring bouts of bronchitis and pleurisy (an inflammation of the lungs) often kept him out of school. His frail health prevented him from engaging in sports and rough- and-tumble games with his friends, so Bob turned to books for companionship. He soon became an avid reader and was often seen at the library, where he scoured the shelves for books on electricity, chemistry, magic, crystals, and the atmosphere.

Bob liked, above all, to read books and articles about space travel, and he discovered, among the treasures in the library, books that were to give direction to his life. He read Edgar Allan Poe's story *Lunar Discoveries*; Joseph Atterlay's *A Voyage to the Moon*; Percy Greg's *Across the Zodiac*; and Edward Everett Hale's *The Brick Moon*. And he read about the celebrated "moon hoax" of 1853, when a series of newspaper articles reported that lunar creatures had been sighted through the telescope of Sir John Herschel, a famous astronomer. The hoax showed how readily people would accept the idea of life on other worlds.

These fantastic stories appealed to Bob's imagination. But it was the books of H. G. Wells, Garrett P. Serviss, and Jules Verne that set his mind racing about the possibilities of space travel. Bob was inspired by Jules Verne's *From the Earth to the Moon*, and sat for hours reading and rereading the book, noting where Verne's fiction deviated from fact and writing his own corrections in the margins. He was undoubtedly struck by the fact that Verne, a Frenchman, set his story in the United States. In describing a group of men who decided to travel to the moon, Verne wrote, "They had all comprehended the idea in an instant, and saw no real difficulty in it. An American sees no real difficulty in anything. . . . In America everything is easy, every-thing is simple . . . engineering difficulties seem to be all still-born. Between [the moon] project and its complete realiza-tion, no true American could see the shadow of a difficulty. To *say* it, meant to *do* it." Bob could see his own philosophy mirrored in these words. To Bob, as to Verne's Americans, all things seemed possible.

Bob found more food for thought when the *Boston Post*, a local newspaper, published, in serial form, *Fighters from Mars or the War of the Worlds, In and Near Boston* by H. G. Wells. Wells's vivid writing set Bob's mind racing about the practical reality of space travel. It was thrilling to imagine alien invaders march-ing down the familiar cobblestoned streets of his own neighbor-hood. It was even more thrilling to imagine that a flight to Mars might be possible. A few months later, another story, Garrett P. Serviss's *Edison's Conquest of Mars*, appeared in the newspaper. Once again, Bob's imagination was gripped by thoughts of space travel.

From his reading, Bob concluded that the main problem facing space travelers was finding a way to propel a spacecraft far enough and fast enough to escape Earth's gravitational pull. Surely, he thought, there must be a solution to the problem. With the kind of sunny confidence that was to characterize him throughout his life, Bob decided that, in the words of Jules Verne, "To *say* it, meant to *do* it." He set up a laboratory in the attic and began to experiment with ways of launching objects into space.

Sometimes Bob's experiments went awry. Once, while trying to see if he could manufacture artificial diamonds, Bob narrowly escaped injury when a glass bottle, in which hydrogen was being generated from zinc, suddenly exploded, sending shards of glass flying through the room with such force that they became imbedded in the door and ceiling. On another occasion, he reasoned correctly that a mixture of hydrogen and oxygen might produce a force strong enough to lift an object into the air. When he tested the theory, he discovered, much to his dismay, that the mixture did produce a powerful force—powerful enough, indeed, to shatter the attic windows—and that hydrogen mixed with oxygen could be dangerous if not handled carefully. As for the broken windows, Bob was fortunate to have forgiving parents who understood and encouraged his interest in science.

Next, Bob turned his attention to lighter-than-air flight. From his reading, he knew about the famous hot-air balloon flight made in 1783 by the Montgolfier brothers. The balloon, carrying two passengers, had traveled seven and one-half miles over Paris and had risen about 330 feet into the air. Since then, other balloonists had attempted to scale the heavens. It seemed only natural to Bob to build a balloon of his own. He recorded his decision to do so in his diary in December, 1897.

An ordinary balloon of silk or rubber would not do; he wanted a permanent balloon, one that would require no refilling. Bob decided to build his balloon of aluminum because of the metal's strength and light weight and because it was inexpensive and available. Eager to test his ideas, he hurried to the hardware store on the morning of Saturday, January 8, 1898, and purchased a half-pound of aluminum. He planned to melt the aluminum and then manufacture thin sheets of the metal from which he would form the balloon. At home, he tried unsuccessfully to melt the aluminum, managing only to put out the fire in the kitchen stove several times.

Unable to reduce the lump of aluminum to a malleable state, Bob knew that another trip to the hardware store was needed—but a week was to pass before he could acquire the necessary funds. His diary entry for January 18 notes that, after school, he purchased three feet of sheet aluminum for 54 cents. In the days that followed, Bob thought of little else. He worked busily after school cutting and shaping the aluminum. On Thursday, January 27, he noted in his diary that he had cemented the aluminum with litharge and glycerin. The pillow-shaped balloon was ready for testing. All he needed was some hydrogen to send it aloft.

Bob explained his problem to Jim Young, the clerk at a local drugstore that stocked canisters of hydrogen. Amused by Bob's earnestness and impressed by his interest in science, Young agreed to pump hydrogen into the balloon at no cost. Flight time, they agreed, would be on Saturday morning, February 19.

A small crowd of people gathered on the sidewalk outside the drugstore and watched with anticipation as Young pumped the lighter-than-air hydrogen into Bob's balloon. Bob had attached a long string to the balloon so that he could retrieve it from flight. He held the end of the string tightly in his hand, expecting a strong tug when the balloon rose. Finally, the balloon was completely filled with hydrogen. But nothing happened. The aluminum sheets were too thick; the balloon had too much weight for the hydrogen to lift. The disappointed crowd dispersed. That night, Bob wrote dejectedly in his diary: "Aluminum balloon will not go up. . . . Failior [sic] crowns enterprise."

After the balloon experiment, Bob once again considered the problem of propelling a spacecraft beyond Earth. After much thought, he concluded that the problem of sending a spacecraft beyond the reach of Earth's gravity might be solved if someone were to invent a super-powerful rocket. He knew that rockets, although they were small devices with little power and limited range, had been used for military purposes since they were first invented by the Chinese in the 13th century. And of course he had seen rockets light up the sky with brilliant pyrotechnic displays on the Fourth of July. The national anthem even immortalized their use, recalling "the rockets' red glare" during the bombardment of Fort McHenry in 1814.

A few months after the failed balloon experiment, two holidays provided Bob with opportunities to engage in some ordinary schoolboy fun while pursuing his scientific interests. On June 17, 1898, he wrote this entry in his diary: "(Flag Day). Fired firecrackers and common crackers. . . . Had rocket, Roman candles, red fire, etc. in evening." And again, on July 4, 1898, Bob's diary notes that he "fired cannon, 'pop,' and firecrackers all day. In evening had 5 skyrockets, 3 Roman candles, 1 large pinwheel, red fire, and a Japanese match which I made."

As always, Bob discussed his ideas with his parents. Nahum Goddard told him that, although most people considered space travel a ridiculous notion, he agreed with Bob that it might someday be possible. But Goddard cautioned his son not to waste his time on haphazard experiments but to concentrate instead on getting a good education. The study of mathematics and science, he advised, would give Bob the grounding he needed in order to achieve his goals; true scientific work depended on these tools.

In September, 1898, Bob entered his first year at Boston's English High School, determined to follow his father's advice. Until then, he had always received poor or unsatisfactory grades in mathematics. "I learned the principles easily enough and secured a wide variety of answers to the long problems in multiplication and division," he wrote years later, "but these answers seldom included the correct solution." Now 16-year-old Bob applied himself diligently to the study of algebra and managed to earn a satisfactory grade.

As the school year drew to a close, Bob looked forward to a summer of reading and thinking about space travel. But events did not go as he planned. Earlier in the year, his mother had fallen ill with pulmonary tuberculosis and, as summer approached, her condition grew worse. The doctor recommended rest and country air, so the Goddard family left the bustling streets of Boston to move back to Worcester, 40 miles away, where Bob's grandmother owned a farmhouse on the edge of town. The Goddards had vacationed there in summers past, but the summer of 1899 proved to be no vacation for either Fannie Goddard or her son.

Several weeks before arriving at the farm, Bob fell ill himself. The doctor diagnosed severe stomach and kidney ailments, and insisted that his young patient remain in bed. Throughout the long summer, Bob followed the doctor's orders. He wanted desperately to get well so that he could resume his studies and experiments. But when September came, Bob was still too sick to move about. Despite his patient's protests, the doctor pronounced him too ill to return to school. Young Bob Goddard was temporarily grounded.

CHAPTER 1 NOTES

p. 1   "It shall be done . . ." Wernher von Braun and Frederick I. Ordway III, *History of Rocketry and Space Travel*, p. 14.

p. 3   "I imagine an innate interest . . ." Esther C. Goddard, Ed., and G. Edward Pendray, Assoc. Ed., *The Papers of Robert H. Goddard*, Vol. I: 1898–1924, p. 7. Note: Hereafter, references to this work will be cited as PRHG, Vol. I, II (1925–37), or III (1938–45).

p. 4   "My father and I . . ." PRHG, Vol. I, p. 4.

p. 6   "They had all comprehended . . ." Jules Verne, *From the Earth to the Moon. All Around the Moon: Space Novels*, trans. Edward Roth, p. 63.

p. 8   "Aluminum balloon will not . . ." PRHG, Vol. I, p. 51.

p. 9   "Fired firecrackers and . . ." PRHG, Vol. I, p. 51.

p. 9   "Fired cannon, 'pop' . . ." PRHG, Vol. I, p. 52.

p. 9   "I learned the principles . . ." PRHG, Vol. I, p. 5.

2

A DIFFERENT BOY

"... the dream of yesterday, is the hope of today and the reality of tomorrow."
—Robert Hutchings Goddard

Although Bob Goddard was not well enough to return to high school when classes resumed in the fall of 1899, his illness did not prevent him from reading, writing, and taking short rambling walks. At Maple Hill, his grandmother's home, he and his parents occupied the rooms on the second floor. He had spent the summer there, confined to his bed for many weeks, and he was tired of being cooped up indoors. Inactivity made him restless and, as autumn began to tint the wooded hills with color, Bob looked for any excuse to go outdoors.

Autumn is always a glorious season in New England, and the autumn of 1899 was no exception. October brought clear blue skies, cool air, and a brilliant landscape that beckoned irresistibly to Bob. One afternoon, he decided to trim the dead limbs of a large cherry tree behind the barn. He leaned a ladder against the tree and, armed with a saw and hatchet, climbed up among the branches.

Seating himself on a high limb, Bob gazed at the lovely scene surrounding him while thoughts about space travel drifted through his mind. He remembered the excitement he had felt years before when he first read the stories of H. G. Wells, Garrett Serviss, and Jules Verne, and he thought again how wonderful it would be to travel to Mars. Surely, it must be possible, he mused, to invent a vehicle that could transport people into space. Then, as his eyes surveyed the beauty of the afternoon, he caught a glimpse of the future and, in a few spellbound moments of rapturous insight, he had an experience that was to change his life.

Years later, he described his experience this way:

> *It was one of those quiet, colorful afternoons of sheer beauty which we have in October in New England, and as I looked toward the fields at the east, I imagined how wonderful it would be to make some device which has even the* possibility *of ascending to Mars, and how it would look on a small scale, if sent up from the meadow at my feet. . . . It seemed to me then that a weight whirling around a horizontal shaft, moving more rapidly above than below, could furnish lift by virtue of the greater centrifugal force at the top of the path. . . . I was a different boy when I descended the tree from when I ascended, for existence at last seemed very purposive.*

The date was October 19, 1899. His experience that afternoon was to remain vivid and alive in Bob Goddard's memory for the

The cherry tree, with Goddard's ladder and saw, at Maple Hill. On October 19, 1899, while seated on a limb of this tree, Robert Goddard decided to devote his life to the exploration of space. This photo was taken by him in 1900. (Goddard Collection/Clark University)

rest of his life. Forever after, he referred to October 19 as "Anniversary Day"—the day on which he first decided to devote himself to the exploration of space.

A few weeks later, while on a trip to Boston with his grandfather, Bob outlined his idea about the use of centrifugal force to his cousin Percy, who was a student at Harvard. Percy said the idea probably wouldn't work if put to the test but could give Bob no convincing reasons why.

Would his idea work? Bob didn't know, but his cousin's inability to give conclusive reasons why it wouldn't made him hopeful. There was only one way to find out. Accordingly, he made several models of the whirling machine he had envisioned—but when he set them in motion, they remained earthbound. It was disappointing to see his idea fail, but it made him realize that having imagination was not enough to accomplish his goals. He would have to apply himself seriously to the study of physics and mathematics if he were ever to invent or discover a way to attain great heights and navigate in space.

Finally, in 1901, Bob was well enough to return to school. With his new sense of purpose spurring him on, Bob entered the sophomore class at South High School in Worcester, firmly resolved to shine in physics and mathematics. Physics, as taught by a capable, inspiring teacher named Calvin H. Andrews, proved to be easy enough for Bob, and he had no difficulty in leading his class in that subject. Mathematics, however, was another story. But Bob was determined to succeed and, as part of his plan, he produced a painstaking book of original geometric propositions. Although some of the propositions were unworkable, the project made geometry a pleasure to think about and, by the end of the school year, Bob led his class in that subject as well.

His years at South High School were happy ones for Bob Goddard. He enjoyed working in the school's well-equipped science laboratories under the guidance of enthusiastic teachers. His classmates knew that the tall, slim teenager was a brilliant student with an intense interest in science, and they predicted that he would amount to something someday, although no one was quite sure what. He could have been shunned as an "oddball" or a "brain," but his shy, modest manner won him the respect and admiration of his fellow students. They welcomed Bob as a friend and elected him class president two years in a row.

About this time, Nahum Goddard purchased a small machine tool factory in Worcester. His partner in this venture was a man named Charles H. Bliss. Both men had sons named Robert, and, although they were very different, the two boys became friends. Years later, Robert Bliss's daughter described her father as "handsome, sociable, and lively," while Bob Goddard was "interested in science and explosives and was reclusive." She recalled that their "two fathers used to say that if you could shake the two Roberts in a bag you might get a normal person."

Although dreams of space travel never left his thoughts, Bob found time to pursue other interests in high school. He studied French, edited the school newspaper, and acted in school plays. He had always loved music and had a fine singing voice, so now he sang in a quartet at school shows and was elected class pianist. At home, he practiced drawing, played the piano, and listened to music on that new-fangled contraption, the phonograph, that his father brought home one day. He attended concerts whenever he could, noting in his diary on each occasion that he had had a "splendid" or an "excellent" time. He formed a few special friendships and acquired a sweetheart, Miriam Olmstead, whom he took to dances and school functions.

Bob's involvement in school and social activities absorbed much of his time, but he had discovered that thinking about many different subjects, instead of concentrating on just one subject, stimulated his mind. In a special notebook labeled "Suggestions," he wrote, "It is a very important thing to jot down suggestions that come into one's mind from time to time, as the thoughts that are most useful do not come at a bidding. . . . If the mind is continually engrossed with one subject, other and perhaps more important suggestions will be excluded. . . . Activity fosters growth and thus furnishes suggestions."

Certainly, Bob's mind was continually active. He knew that a mastery of mathematics was essential, since mathematics is the language of science. And the more he studied science at school, the more he realized that all branches of science depended on one another and that all of them were relevant to his goals. For instance, the things he learned in his physics class helped him to understand chemistry, and the knowledge he gained in his chemistry class helped him to understand physics.

Bob found that even the life sciences could be relevant to his interests. While studying human physiology, he discovered that a small structure in the inner ear controls the sense of balance. Did birds in flight maintain their balance in the same way, he wondered? Someday, rockets would need a balancing device to keep them on course, and maybe a study of birds would give him the clues he needed to build such a device. He sat outdoors for hours watching the aerial acrobatics of chimney swifts in flight, carefully noting how those remarkable birds used their wings and tails to steer a course as they glided through the air. From his observations, Bob concluded that the perfect flying machine of the future would have little use for a tail, but would need wings with flaps that could be adjusted upward or downward to maintain balance. In his notebook, he sketched out plans for a balancing mechanism that would automatically adjust the wing flaps. Like several other ideas he had at the time, this idea was to bear fruit in later years.

In his spare time, Bob pored over issues of *Scientific American* and *Popular Science News*, always alert to information that might be useful to him. In a series of files that reflected the methodical orderliness of his mind, he carefully arranged notes and articles on subjects that were of special interest to him.

Writing in his notebooks was, by now, a daily habit with Bob. He kept detailed notes of his ideas and plans and made a daily record of his progress. Not all of the comments in his notebooks, however, dealt with ideas or experiments. He wrote about riding a bicycle, seeing President Theodore Roosevelt (twice!) at the Worcester City Hall, rehearsing with the quartet in which he was a singer, seeing a motor car, riding a trolley, going to a concert by John Philip Sousa, raking leaves, trimming trees, taking photographs, escorting Miriam to a school dance, attending plays, seeing his friends, watching an eclipse, flying kites, and shooting rockets on the Fourth of July. His enthusiastic comments about these and scores of similar events clearly reveal that Bob was a young man who regarded life with optimism and whose active mind took great joy in the world around him.

Every phenomenon of nature was interesting to Bob. Once, on a hot summer evening, it seemed to him that the crickets were chirping more noisily than usual, and he wondered if their chirping was influenced by the weather. For several weeks, he carefully noted their activity and drew up a chart showing that there was, indeed, a correlation between evening temperatures and the frequency and loudness of cricket chirps.

At the library, Bob found books on acoustics, wireless telegraphy, and electricity. He immediately put his new knowledge to the test by building a telegraph system between the house and the barn. After trying it out with a friend, he wrote in his notebook, "Works fine." But no matter what other interests he pursued, Bob's thoughts always returned to space travel. He continued to theorize about new ways to propel objects into space and was careful, as always, to record his ideas in his notebooks.

During the Christmas holidays in 1901, Bob wrote a brief article entitled "The Navigation of Space" in which he discussed the dangers that meteors would pose to spacecraft, as well as the difficulties that might be expected if one were to use a series of cannons nested inside one another—each cannon to fire a successively smaller one—to launch a spacecraft. Inspired by one of Jules Verne's ideas, Bob's notion of employing propulsion units that operate in sequence anticipated the principle of the multistage rocket. He ended the article with this statement: "We may safely infer that space navigation is an impossibility at the present time; yet it is difficult to predict the achievements of science in this direction in the distant future." Bob's later writings and statements were sprinkled with similar cautions. Although he believed privately that rockets would someday allow humans to explore the solar system, he was always reluctant to advance claims about ideas that had not been tested and proven scientifically.

Bob submitted the article to *Popular Science News*, but the editor sent the 19-year-old author a polite letter of rejection. He wrote more articles and submitted them to science magazines, but none were published. Although they were well-written, the articles all managed to raise more questions than they answered.

Nothing, however, seemed to deflate Bob's spirits. If one idea failed, he eagerly tried out a new one. During his last two years of high school, he spent a lot of time developing plans for a propulsion system based on a "machine-gun" device that would send objects aloft by firing bullets downward. Although, in the end, this system proved to be unworkable, another idea he had at that time was eventually more profitable.

Bob's notebook shows that on October 19, 1902 ("Anniversary Day"), he "sat in cherry tree in afternoon and slung apples." He didn't record what he thought about that day, but sitting in the tree always seemed to fuel his imagination. A few days later his notebook entry shows that he began experimenting with a gyroscope.

Ever since watching the chimney swifts, Bob had wondered what kind of device might be used to control rockets in flight. Now, he wondered if a toy gyroscope top held the answer. Originally devised to illustrate the rotation of the Earth, gyroscopes had no special use at the turn of the century but were considered curiosities—unusual toys for children. Once a gyroscope top is sent spinning and moving in one direction, it will continue moving in the same direction even if you try to make it move in a different direction. If it is spinning with enough force, any effort to push it over will fail. The gyroscope will pop back to an upright position and continue on its course.

Fascinated by the gyroscope's ability to remain in one plane and one direction, Bob experimented with it, hoping to show that its persistent force could be harnessed to propel a rocket. The experiment was a failure, but he recorded the results in his notebook anyway. Then he envisioned a mechanism, using gyroscopes set at right angles to one another, that could be used to counteract any forces that tried to push the rocket off course. The force produced by the resistance of the gyroscopes could be used to trigger a device that would set the rocket back on course. Again, he recorded his ideas in his notebook. At the time, Bob considered his experiments with gyroscopes to be failures, but years later, he would look back and realize that the germs of some very good ideas had been contained in those youthful experiments.

Thoughts of gyroscopes were temporarily driven from Bob's mind after he attended a lecture about butterflies. With characteristic enthusiasm, he set about collecting specimens and preparing microscope slides of their wing scales. He discovered that it was possible to classify butterflies by observing their tiny scales.

Bob found so many subjects fascinating that it was hard for him to decide which avenue to pursue. However, now in his senior year in high school, Bob realized that it was time to settle on plans for his future. More than anything, he wanted to follow his dreams of building rockets and traveling in space, but his teachers urged him to consider a more earthbound career. They pointed out that there was no "science" of rocketry, no rocket industry, and certainly no full-time jobs for rocket inventors. Besides, they said, the whole notion of rocketry was silly and impractical.

Bob was an outstanding student who did well in all his subjects. His teachers predicted that he would do well in any course of study that he chose to follow. Because of the ability and creativity Bob had demonstrated in writing essays and short stories, one of his teachers even suggested that he pursue a career in literature. In the end, he decided to study science and engineering at Worcester Polytechnic Institute, where he could prepare for some sort of job in science. He might even become a teacher. But no matter what path he followed, Bob believed that a "practical education, from an economic standpoint at least, should tend to develop what is best in a man and to make him as useful a unit as possible in the community."

When his senior year at South High School drew to a close, Bob was chosen to give a speech at the graduation exercises. The subject he chose was "On Taking Things for Granted." After talking about several advances in science that had at first seemed impossible, and cautioning his audience that it is "dangerous to believe hastily that anything is either possible or impossible," he concluded with the thought that "no one can predict to what heights of wealth, fame, or usefulness he may rise until he has honestly endeavored . . . and that it has often proved true that the dream of yesterday is the hope of today and the reality of tomorrow."

Bob's own dream, however, didn't look very promising. "By the time I graduated from high school," he later wrote, "I had a set of models which would not work and a number of suggestions which, from the physics I had learned, I now knew were erroneous." One Sunday morning, he gathered up his notes and burned them in the little old-fashioned wood stove that sat in his grandmother's dining room.

Fortunately, Bob's feeling of discouragement didn't last long. Within a few months, his mind churned with new ideas. "The dream would not down," he said, "and inside of two months I caught myself making notes of further suggestions, for even though I reasoned with myself that the thing was impossible, there was something inside which simply would not stop working." Indeed, for the rest of his life, that "something inside" would never stop working. He bought a fresh set of notebooks and immediately began to record his new ideas systematically.

In the fall of 1904, Bob Goddard enrolled in the general science program at Worcester Polytechnic Institute. His main interest, however, was physics. Physics, he was sure, held the key to space travel; if people were ever to discover or invent a way to navigate in space, it would be through an understanding and application of that science.

Back in high school, Bob had been told repeatedly that the idea of space travel was a lunatic notion best left to writers of fiction. Now at Worcester Tech, as the school was called, Bob was careful to keep his speculations to himself. But he was hungry for knowledge that might solve the problems that filled his mind. In class, he bombarded his professors with questions. However, when they, in turn, asked him what had sparked his curiosity, he gave distant, evasive answers that held no clues to his real interest. Nearly all his life, Bob would remain a loner, working privately and keeping his dreams to himself. Only in his later years would he reveal his vision to others, and then only to a few trusted friends.

At Worcester Polytechnic Institute, with its excellent faculty, Bob was finally getting the advanced scientific training he needed. He studied hard and proved to be a brilliant student. For an English assignment in his freshman year, he wrote a fascinating paper entitled "Traveling in 1950," in which he outlined plans for a rapid transit system to run between Boston and New York. The traveler would be transported in an airtight car that would travel through a vacuum tunnel. The car would ride above, and out of contact with, the roadbed, and would be propelled by the action of electromagnets embedded in the walls and bottom of both the car and the tunnel. During the first half of the journey, the car would accelerate to a maximum speed of 1,200 miles per hour, and it would decelerate by an equal amount during the second half of the journey. Altogether, the trip would take only 10 minutes! His astonished classmates thought it was a capital idea, and his professors, although dubious about its practicality, could find no fault with Bob's calculations or with his scientific reasoning. Later, Bob incorporated this idea of a magnetic transportation system into a short story entitled "The High Speed Bet," which was eventually published in 1914.

Referring back to his studies of chimney swifts and gyroscopes, Bob wrote another essay in which he suggested using gyroscopes to balance airplanes in flight and bending their wings to aid in steering. He revised the essay and, in 1907 (only a few years after the Wright brothers' first powered airplane test), it was published by *Scientific American* as "The Use of the Gyroscope in the Balancing and Steering of Airplanes."

During his freshman year, Bob tackled his courses with enthusiasm. He was sure that somewhere in his studies he would find the clues that would help him solve the mysteries of space flight. At the end of 1904, he wrote in his diary, "Anything is possible with the man who makes the best use of every minute of his time." And, again, "There are limitless opportunities open to the man who appreciates the fact that his own mind is the sole key that unlocks them." A few months later, in February 1905, he wrote, "If there is no law against it, why—then 'twill happen some day."

Bob continued to work hard throughout his years at Worcester Polytechnic Institute, but he found time, as he had in high school, to pursue other interests. He edited the school newspaper, sang with the glee club, and even composed the school song. In the school yearbook, one classmate described Bob as "a sharp-witted youth, grave, thoughtful, and reserved among his mates, turning hours of sport and food to labor, starving his body to inform his mind." Another friend wrote, "The word 'shark' fails to convey any idea of his appetite for knowledge, for he fairly revels in the weirdest of physics and kindred stumbling blocks to the less fortunate of us. . . . He has been President, Vice President, and Secretary of the class, and a member of committees galore, where his good judgment and untiring effort have been of the greatest value."

Despite all his other activities, Bob's thoughts never strayed far from his dream. In 1907, long before the idea occurred to other scientists and at a time when such an idea would have been considered ludicrous, he wrote about the potential uses of atomic energy, predicting that someday the energy generated from nuclear substances would power rockets in space. His professor, however, told him that the idea was impracticable and of "no use."

Doubts began to creep into his mind and, for a while, Bob's faith in his dream wavered. Would he ever be able to solve the problems involved in space flight, he wondered? There was so much he had yet to learn, so much he had yet to discover. And in the end, would he find success—or would all his hard work result in dismal failure? Feeling frustrated and discouraged, Bob wrote in his diary, "Decided today [March 4, 1906] that space navigation is a physical impossibility."

But his discouragement did not last. Before long, optimism bubbled up inside him and, as it was to do many times throughout his life, Bob Goddard's vision rose before him, beckoning him on. He would devote his life to his quest, and someday, perhaps, he would touch the stars.

Soon after, in a paper entitled "On the Possibility of Navigating Interplanetary Space," Bob outlined the problems facing would-be space travelers: how to sustain life in space, how to protect against accidents during transit, and the means of propulsion. He submitted the paper to *Popular Astronomy*, but the editor rejected it with the comment, "The speculation about it is interesting, but the impossibility of ever doing it is so certain that it is not practically useful. You have written well and clearly, but not helpfully to science as I see it."

Again, Bob refused to be discouraged. Vowing to pick up the pieces and keep trying, he wrote an article that gave instructions for constructing an inexpensive astronomical telescope and sent it off to *Scientific American*. This time, the editor wrote to say that his work was accepted and enclosed a check for 10 dollars in payment.

On June 11, 1908, Bob Goddard graduated from Worcester Polytechnic Institute with high grades and a Bachelor of Science degree. "Got first prize, $75," he wrote in his diary. But a degree was not all he had to show for his four years of work. He also had a set of personal notebooks filled with scores of remarkable ideas, including plans for a solar energy device that would harness the sun's rays to power spaceships in space, and speculations on ion propulsion—a method for using a beam of tiny accelerated particles to give thrust—that is now considered especially suitable for long-distance space missions.

Bob looked forward to entering Clark University, also located in Worcester, where he hoped to work toward advanced degrees. Unfortunately, his plans had to be postponed. Funds were short in the Goddard household that year; there was simply no money to pay for tuition at Clark. He decided, instead, to accept the offer of a teaching job at Worcester Polytechnic Institute. The salary was $850 a year, just enough to allow him to scrape by. It was a temporary setback, but one that he accepted with his usual grace. At the end of 1908, he wrote in his diary, "The years forever fashion new dreams, when old ones go. God pity a one-dream man."

Now 25 years old, Bob Goddard was a tall, thin, handsome young man with a kind face and intense dark eyes that sparkled with intelligence. He was anxious to get on with his work, and this delay was disappointing. But he had overcome delays caused by illness in the past, and he would overcome this money problem, too. Bob Goddard's dreams would see him through.

CHAPTER 2 NOTES

p. 11   " . . . the dream of yesterday. . ." From "On Taking Things for Granted," Robert Goddard's graduation oration at South High School, Worcester, Mass., June 24, 1904. Appears in PRHG, Vol. I, p. 66.

p. 12   "It was one of those quiet . . ." PRHG, Vol. I, p. 9.

p. 14   "two fathers used to say . . ." From a letter sent to the author by Barbara Bliss Peck, granddaughter of Charles H. Bliss, who was Nahum Goddard's partner in the L. Hardy Company, Worcester, Massachusetts, and whose father, Robert Bliss, was Robert Goddard's friend. In speaking of her father in later years, Peck said that

Robert Bliss "never lost respect for the genius of his old friend."

p. 14   "It is a very important thing . . ." PRHG, Vol. I, p. 61.
p. 16   "Works fine" PRHG, Vol. I, p. 60.
p. 16   "We may safely infer . . ." PRHG, Vol. I, p. 57.
p. 17   "sat in cherry tree . . ." PRHG, Vol. I, p. 60.
p. 18   "practical education . . ." PRHG, Vol. I, p. 68.
p. 18   "dangerous to believe hastily . . ." PRHG, Vol. I, p. 66.
p. 18   "By the time I graduated . . ." PRHG, Vol. I, p. 22.
p. 19   "The dream would not down . . ." PRHG, Vol. I, p. 11.
p. 20   "Anything is possible . . ." PRHG, Vol. I, p. 68.
p. 20   "If there is no law against it . . ." PRHG, Vol. I, p. 69.
p. 20   "A sharp-witted youth . . ." PRHG, Vol. I, p. 88.
p. 20   "The word shark . . ." PRHG, Vol. I, p. 88.
p. 21   "Decided today . . ." PRHG, Vol. I, p. 74.
p. 21   "The speculation about it . . ." PRHG, Vol. I, p. 88.
p. 22   "Got first prize . . ." PRHG, Vol. I, p. 88.
p. 22   "The years forever fashion . . ." PRHG, Vol. I, p. 95.

3

NEWTON'S LAW

"To every action there is always opposed an equal reaction: or the mutual actions of two bodies upon each other are always equal, and directed to contrary parts."
—Sir Isaac Newton

While still in high school, Goddard had pored over the writings of Sir Isaac Newton, the great 17-century physicist, and had wondered if Newton's principles could be applied to solving some of the practical problems of space travel. Newton's Third Law, in particular, fired the imagination of the thoughtful teenager. Stated simply, this principle says that *for every action there is an equal and opposite reaction.* A practical demonstration of this principle occurs whenever a child, playing with an ordinary balloon, fills it with air and then releases it. The balloon exerts pressure on the air inside it; the air then rushes out, and the balloon, in *reaction*, is propelled forward in an erratic, often amusing flight. Another example of this principle in action occurs when a firefighter holds the nozzle of a fire hose through which water is flowing under great pressure. The force of the water gushing out in one direction causes the nozzle to push in the opposite direction. To fight the *reaction* of the nozzle, the firefighter must apply an equal amount of force by bracing his or her body and using physical strength to prevent the hose from moving backward.

The more Goddard thought about it, the more he was convinced that Newton's reaction principle held the key to sending rockets aloft. It was an important insight, and Goddard's subsequent development of the idea was fundamental to the success of space flight and jet travel. Today's jet planes are propelled forward by the hot air and gases rushing out of the rear of their engines. Rockets are launched and propelled in much the same way.

By the time he was in his senior year at Worcester Polytechnic Institute, Goddard had begun experimenting secretly with the idea. It wasn't always easy, however, to hide his work from others. On one occasion, his activities became the talk of the school when he ignited a rocket in the basement and filled the building with smoke. His excited classmates wanted to know what Goddard was up to, but he managed to explain away the incident without revealing his true purpose.

In 1909, while teaching at Worcester Tech, Goddard continued to formulate his ideas. Working late at night and in whatever spare time he could muster, he labored over the basic mathematics of rocket propulsion, developed a skeleton plan for a multiple- stage, or step, rocket, and outlined a theory for using explosive jets fueled with hydrogen and oxygen to obtain lift. These revolutionary ideas were the seeds from which the science of rocketry grew. Today, for instance, hydrogen and oxygen are commonly used in liquid-fuel rockets, but at the time, no one—except Bob Goddard—had imagined their potential. From his calculations, Goddard knew that a combination of liquid hydrogen and liquid oxygen would yield a much greater amount of energy per unit of weight than any other fuel. Alone, with no resources except for his own intelligence and resolution, and with scanty funds, Goddard had taken the first bold steps on a journey that would lead humankind to the stars.

After a year of teaching at Worcester Polytechnic Institute, Goddard had saved enough money to enroll at Clark University. Because Clark was conveniently located in Worcester, he was able to keep his expenses to a minimum by continuing to live at home, as he had done while attending Worcester Tech.

Economy, however, was the least of the reasons for attending Clark. When Goddard became a student in September 1909, the university's well-equipped science department boasted an outstanding faculty that included several famous and soon-to-be famous scientists. A. A. Michelson, who won the 1907 Nobel Prize in physics, and Ernest Rutherford, who won the 1908 Nobel Prize in chemistry, both taught at Clark, along with physicists Vito Volterra and Robert Williams Wood.

Inspired and encouraged by his professors, Goddard grew more confident and determined than ever. His confidence was accompanied by a growing awareness of the correlation between the physical universe and his own dreams and destiny. His diary for December 1909 contains this entry: "The most wonderful thing in nature is the uniformity, that $2 + 2 = 4$, and that all the atoms of the same element are alike—and the constant development toward higher perfection, even if temporal and at times uncertain. . . . The most amazing thing is that there *is* a tendency toward evolution and development. Since there is, we have our duty defined now. This is the thing to guide us. . . ." More than ever, he believed that someday the problems of space flight could be solved and that solving these problems was, for him, a moral imperative. He knew that long years of work lay ahead, but his vision was clear and his determination was firm. After a visit to his beloved cherry tree on October 19, 1910 (Anniversary Day), he wrote, "See it through. Be the one that will find what can be done. . ."

Two years of hard study earned Goddard both his master's degree (1910) and his doctorate in physics (1911), under the guidance of Arthur G. Webster, a famous mathematical physicist. After Goddard's oral examinations for his doctoral, Dr. Webster told him, "You did yourself proud, and everybody connected with you." Another professor, Dr. Taber, told him, "I was proud to know that one of my students could have such a grasp of his subject," and yet another praised him for being "very brilliant." He had truly earned the right to be addressed as Dr. Robert Goddard. It was a proud, happy day for Goddard—but all his hard work suddenly caught up with him. He felt exhausted. So, on the following day, he celebrated by doing something he had never done before: he slept through the entire day and did not wake until late in the evening.

Goddard wrote as his thesis "On Some Peculiarities of Electrical Conductivity Exhibited by Powders and a Few Solid Substances," a subject in which he was not particularly interested. His professors told him that, on the basis of this work, he could have carved out a career in the new field of radio—but that was not what he wanted. What mattered most to him were the ideas he had developed and the knowledge he had gained working on his own while at Clark.

By the time he finished his studies at the university, Goddard had a stack of notebooks filled with extraordinary ideas, including plans for an airplane that would operate at high speed by the repulsion of charged particles, propulsion in space by repulsion of charged particles, the use of airplanes on rockets, the use of jets, and a method for producing hydrogen and oxygen on the moon. His ideas about breaking up atoms by the impact of ions (charged particles) shooting at very high speeds had led him to experiment with ions moving in closed paths inside vacuum tubes. A few years later, in 1915, he patented his findings as a "Method and Means for Producing Electrically Charged Particles." His experiments with another important idea, that of obtaining forced vibrations of any desired frequency by means of an oscillating cathode-ray beam, resulted in a patent as well.

After receiving his doctorate, Goddard was invited to spend an additional year at Clark as an honorary fellow in physics. Both Columbia University in New York and the University of Missouri had offered him well-paying jobs, but Goddard decided to turn them down in favor of remaining at Clark, where he had access to the laboratories and the advice of the faculty.

It was a happy, productive year. With the pressure of classes and exams lifted, Goddard found more time to pursue other interests. He attended concerts and plays with friends. He traveled to Washington, D.C., to attend a meeting of the American Association for the Advancement of Science and, after attending lectures about new developments in the study of light waves and electricity, he toured the National Museum, the Smithsonian Institution, the Bureau of Standards, the Weather Bureau, and the Library of Congress. He even found time to enjoy a "moving-picture show." A few months later, he delivered a paper on electricity and magnetism at a meeting of the American Physical Society at Harvard University.

In June, 1912, Goddard received the exciting news that he had received a one-year research fellowship at Princeton University in New Jersey for work in electricity, magnetism, infrared, and electron theory. The future looked bright, indeed, for the young physicist, and his mind churned with new ideas. That summer, he spent his evenings writing notes and outlines for further work on the problems of space flight: how to protect spacecraft from meteors, how to control acceleration, the physiological effects of acceleration, making instruments to record information during altitude trials, using cameras to record flights to and around planets, how to return an orbiting spacecraft to Earth, the pros and cons of using solid propellants versus liquid or gas propellants, using electricity as a propellant in space, using solar energy, and how to raise heavy objects to great heights.

When September came, Goddard journeyed to Princeton in time to witness the excitement surrounding the November election of Woodrow Wilson, former president of the university, to the presidency of the United States. Goddard was charmed by the quiet town and by the beautiful buildings and large, old trees on the university campus, but he allowed himself little time to enjoy his new surroundings. During the day, he worked on displacement-current experiments, with the doors and windows sealed up and a hydrogen generator spewing sulfuric acid fumes into the lab. When evening came, he could hardly wait to resume work on his theory of rocket propulsion—the problem that was foremost in his mind. His excitement grew because he was proving, mathematically at least, how a small amount of smokeless powder, or hydrogen and oxygen fuel, could lift a rocket into space. The problem was so engrossing that he often found that he had worked the whole night through.

Goddard's health had always been precarious, so it was inevitable that the long hours and hard work would take their toll. He was bothered by colds that winter, and when Easter vacation rolled around, he returned to Worcester with what he thought was yet another slight cold. His mother, using an old family remedy, applied a mixture of snuff and lard to his chest, but it did no good. The family doctor was called and, after seeing Goddard, he returned with a specialist. Both men shook their heads gravely as they told Goddard that he had tuberculosis of both lungs. Privately, they told Bob's parents that he had two weeks to live.

In the days before antibiotics, tuberculosis was often a fatal disease. The only "cure" was complete rest, with no excitement or activity. Rest allowed the body to fight and hopefully arrest the disease, but, even then, it might recur if the person was again put under physical stress. But Goddard could think only of the project he had left behind at Princeton. "Shall I ever be able to do much work?" he asked. "Some outside work, if you are careful," the doctor replied. Bob immediately asked that all his belongings, including every scrap of paper, be sent to him from Princeton.

A nurse was hired to watch over Goddard. For several weeks, he was forced to remain in bed, unable to do anything. After a month, he was allowed to get out of bed and sit in a chair. After two months, he was allowed to take short walks. When May came, he was allowed to work for one hour every afternoon. With characteristic diligence, he put that hour to good use. By the end of the month, he had produced the material for two U.S. patents that covered the essentials of rocket propulsion. He sent the material off to Washington, D.C., and the following year, in July 1914, the patents were issued.

These two patents deserve special attention because, as Goddard later said, "they give as nearly as possible an answer to the question as to what the 'Goddard Rocket' is." The patents outlined plans for a multiple-charge solid-propellant rocket; a liquid-propellant rocket; a step, or multistage, rocket; an exhaust nozzle to funnel off escaping gases; and a method for sending fuel into a rocket's combustion chamber. Because his experiments using different types of propellants with small-scale rocket models and his use of various methods of feeding fuel into the combustion chambers had proven successful in varying degrees, he did not want to limit the patents to one plan or method. Instead, the patents cover three broad principles of successful rockets: the use of a combustion chamber and nozzle; the feeding of successive portions of liquid or solid propellant into the combustion chamber to give either a steady or an intermittent propulsive force; and, finally, the use of multiple stage, or step, rockets, which can be successively discarded as the fuel that each contains is burned up.

The idea of the multiple stage, or step, rocket overcame one of the main problems of space flight: how to launch a heavy rocket and keep the most important part of it in flight. To provide the initial lift necessary to send a large rocket aloft, a huge amount of fuel and

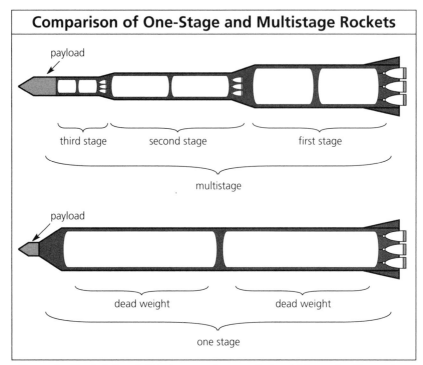

Comparison of One-Stage and Multistage Rockets

payload

third stage   second stage   first stage

multistage

payload

dead weight   dead weight

one stage

Figure 1: **The total weight of a one-stage rocket, which carries its engine and all the fuel in one section, prevents it both from carrying a proportionately large payload and from attaining high altitude. In contrast, the multistage rocket has a series of engines and fuel tanks that can be successively jettisoned as the rocket travels upward, allowing it to carry a heavier payload. All of today's rockets are multistage ("step") rockets.**

equipment are needed. Goddard's calculations showed that if a rocket were to carry its engine and all its fuel in one main section, its weight would prevent the rocket from attaining high altitudes. Goddard reasoned that if the rocket could discard this extra weight soon after launching, it would be able to travel much further. After the heavy section of the rocket was jettisoned, a smaller engine could then take over. This section could, in turn, be discarded as well. Once the rocket had traveled beyond the Earth's atmosphere, it would no longer need the engine for propulsion. Today's rockets follow this design. Sections of the rockets are jettisoned at various altitudes so that the most important part of the rocket—that which carries the astronauts or scientific equipment—is able to travel unencumbered in space.

On May 25, 1913, Goddard was finally allowed to have dinner downstairs with the family. He was delighted to find the dining room decorated with Princeton banners and a toy tiger (the Princeton mascot) sitting on the table as a centerpiece. Even the family dog was decked out in orange and black ribbons, the Princeton colors. It was a happy moment for Goddard. He was surrounded by a warm, loving family; he had proved the doctors' predictions wrong; and he had just accepted the offer of a part-time teaching job at Clark University for the 1914–15 school year. After dinner, an aunt and uncle who were on hand to help celebrate the occasion took Goddard for his first ride in an automobile.

Throughout the fall and winter of 1913 and the spring of 1914, Goddard was able to take daily walks through the wooded hills surrounding the new house that his father had built on a hilltop close to the old family home on Maple Hill. As he walked, his mind surged with new ideas. He began work on a paper entitled "The Navigation of Interplanetary Space" in which he argued that space travel would someday be necessary to ensure the continuance of the human race, and that the moon could be used as a way-station to the more distant planets.

On September 1, 1914, Goddard began work as a part-time physics instructor at Clark, with an annual salary of $500. He had to live frugally, but a light teaching schedule gave him lots of spare time, which he put to good use by working on his own theories in the university's basement laboratories. His figures showed that it was possible to build a 200-pound rocket capable of propelling a one-pound payload beyond the Earth's atmosphere and out into space. After refining his calculations for the use of smokeless powder and of hydrogen and oxygen as rocket fuels, he decided it was time to put his ideas to the test. He had figured out how much fuel would be needed to generate the force necessary to send a small rocket aloft. Now he wanted to find an efficient way to burn the fuel and to harness the force it generated. He decided to use ordinary rockets for his first experiments.

The only kind of rockets that were manufactured at that time were small rockets used by ships to send signals while at sea, and Coston rockets, which were used to carry lifelines to ships in distress. Goddard purchased a few of these ship rockets for his first tests.

Although Goddard's calculations showed that hydrogen and oxygen would be the best fuels to use for interplanetary flights, these powerful propellants were much too complicated and dangerous to use at this early stage. Gunpowder, on the other hand, was inefficient, even though it had been used to fuel rockets ever since they were first invented by the Chinese. So, for these initial experiments, Goddard decided to use smokeless powder, a fuel that had never before been tried in rockets. His goal was to increase the force given off by the powder and thereby increase the velocity at which the gases were ejected. To keep track of the results, he built a measuring apparatus and a frame in which to hold the rockets and prevent them from taking off.

After packing the powder into several ship rockets, Goddard set them off in the basement at Clark. The rockets didn't perform very well, so he began the work of redesigning and improving them. Then, one evening after the students had gone home, he launched a rocket from a shed next to the lab. The main result of this experiment was that he scared the school janitor, who came running to see what had caused the powerful blast and the brightly colored plume of smoke. To avoid arousing any more alarm, Goddard decided to confine himself from then on to static tests in the lab.

To obtain a more powerful explosive force, Goddard reasoned, the powder would have to be under greater pressure. So he devised a means of packing the powder tighter and tested it with another rocket. The time, the result was more successful. "It went!" he wrote in his diary, adding that the blast scattered plaster around the room.

The more Goddard experimented, the more he learned. Finally, he was ready for some outdoor tests. In an open field on the outskirts of Worcester, he launched several small rockets over a nearby lake. Some of the rockets reached a speed of about 1,000 feet per second and attained an altitude of 500 feet before they succumbed to the pull of gravity and fell back to Earth.

Goddard had managed to send ship rockets farther than they had ever traveled before, but they were limited because of the inefficient way they burned fuel. To overcome this problem, he built a steel combustion chamber in the laboratory and fitted it with exhaust nozzles of various sizes. He carefully measured the variations in force that could be generated by using different sizes of nozzles. This time, his experiments yielded remarkable results: the gases were ejected from the nozzle at an average velocity of 7,000 feet per second.

Goddard was sure that if he could build a rocket powerful enough to ascend beyond the stratosphere (the upper portion of the atmosphere that surrounds the Earth), the thrust provided by its engine would allow it to be propelled easily in space. With the pull of gravity lessened, and without the resistance of the Earth's atmosphere to retard its progress, such a rocket could reach the moon and beyond. Many scientists, however, were of the opinion that Newton's Third Law would not work in a vacuum. (A vacuum is a space that contains absolutely nothing, not even air.) If they were right, then a rocket couldn't operate in a vacuum and, therefore, without any atmosphere to push against, the rocket's thrust wouldn't work in outer space.

But Goddard was convinced that the reaction principle outlined in Newton's Third Law was complete in itself and, therefore, the reaction that took place in a rocket did not need atmosphere to push against. The backward thrust caused by the rocket's engine would be enough to propel it forward, in much the same way as a shotgun will "kick" when it is fired. To put his belief to the test, Goddard built a vacuum chamber in the laboratory and conducted a series of tests that proved his theory conclusively. Not only did the rocket engine operate in a vacuum, it produced even greater thrust than it did in the atmosphere.

Except for his family and a few colleagues at Clark University, no one paid much attention to the young inventor or his experiments. As he was to do throughout his life, Goddard worked quietly on his projects. His days were spent teaching classes in physics. He was an enthusiastic, inspiring teacher who enjoyed sharing his knowledge and who often delighted his students with carefully devised and often dramatic classroom demonstrations. It was easy to learn from someone who loved the subject as much as Bob Goddard did, and who believed in guiding, instead of directing, his students to an understanding of physics. The daily interchange with his students was rewarding to Goddard, too, and the pleasure it gave him is reflected in comments he wrote in his diary: "The class yelled afterward!" and "The class cheered!"

After classes, Goddard spent almost every waking hour on his projects. Nearly every evening, and sometimes far into the night, he worked in the lab, testing his theories and ironing out the flaws. Even in sleep, his mind dwelt on space travel. His diary entry for August 8, 1915, reads, "Dreamed . . . of going to the moon, and interested, going and coming, on where going to land respectively on moon and earth. . . . Was cold, and not enough oxygen density to breathe. . . . Saw and took photos of earth with small Kodak while there."

Alone, with no help, Goddard managed to do work that today requires whole teams of scientists and vast financial resources. He had to be his own specialist in metallurgy, aerodynamics, and thermodynamics, as well as a structural, mechanical, and hydraulic engineer.

As for financial resources, he had only himself to rely on. In September 1915, Goddard was promoted to an assistant professorship of physics and his salary was raised to $1,000 per year. It was sufficient to provide the necessities of life but hardly enough to fund the research in which he was engaged. By practicing strict frugality, he managed to stretch his limited funds as far as possible. With amazing ingenuity, he built his own equipment, adapting bits and pieces of discarded machinery to his own uses, and spending only what was necessary to purchase the metals and explosives he needed for his experiments. His engaging, modest personality helped him secure the assistance of others. He drew careful diagrams of parts he needed for his rockets and persuaded the machinists at his father's company to make them for him. A local industrial laboratory tested gunpowder mixtures for him free of charge. "It was almost impossible to turn him down," the owner said. "We ran off his test, not knowing what he was up to, but feeling sure he did."

Goddard did indeed know what he was up to, and the success of his recent experiments convinced him that he was on the right track. He had proved that a rocket would work in a vacuum, he had measured the effect that nozzle design had on the thrust generated by various fuels, and he had worked on perfecting the efficiency of the exhaust nozzle so that maximum thrust could be obtained. He was eager to move on to more elaborate tests, but he needed more materials and equipment. His previous experiments had eaten up his scanty funds. Unless he could find financial support, his work would have to remain at a standstill.

On Goddard's list of possible funding sources was the venerable Smithsonian Institution in Washington, D.C. Founded in 1846 "for the increase and diffusion of knowledge among men," the traditionally conservative Smithsonian seemed an unlikely place from which a scientist with radical ideas might expect to receive support. Undaunted, Goddard wrote a lengthy letter to the president of the Smithsonian asking for help. Careful not to reveal the true purpose of his experiments, he explained that for a number of years he had been working on "a method of raising [atmospheric] recording apparatus to altitudes exceeding the limit for sounding balloons." He mentioned the success he had achieved in static tests with rocket motors, suggested that rockets could be invaluable in gathering atmospheric and meteorological data, included some of his calculations, and asked if the Smithsonian would be willing to underwrite the expense of further experiments.

A few weeks later, Goddard received an encouraging letter from Dr. Charles D. Wolcott, secretary of the Smithsonian, asking for more details and adding, "We are greatly interested in a number of problems that possibly might be solved by the use of your method." Dr. Wolcott also asked how much a high-altitude rocket might cost—a question that several governments since then have spent billions of dollars to answer.

During the summer of 1916, Goddard had written a paper titled "A Method of Reaching Extreme Altitudes," which included all the relevant details and calculations of his experiments. He promptly bound the manuscript, packed it in a wooden box, and sent it to Dr. Wolcott. It was harder for Goddard to come up with a figure for costs. After much careful estimation, he concluded that he would need $10,000 to continue his work, but he was afraid that he would be turned down if he asked for so large a sum. With some hesitation, he wrote, "I do not think that the work I have outlined could possibly be done within a time as short as one year for less than $5,000."

On January 8, 1917, Goddard received a letter saying that his request had been granted. Enclosed was a check for $1,000 to get him started. Goddard was elated, and so were his parents. That evening, he wrote in his diary, "Read letter to Ma and Pa . . . Pa said, 'You certainly put it up to them in wonderful shape.' Ma said, 'I think that's the most wonderful thing I ever heard of. Think of it! You send the Government some typewritten sheets and some pictures, and they send you $1,000, and tell you they are going to send four more.'" It was not a large sum, but it was enough for Bob Goddard to begin in earnest to realize his dreams.

Eager to start development and construction of a large solid-fuel rocket, Goddard made arrangements to use the laboratories at both Worcester Polytechnic Institute and Clark University. His aim was to produce a rocket that would have a large amount of propellant in proportion to total weight, and his plans called for using smokeless powder as the propellant because it posed the least difficulties in experiments.

Goddard had barely completed a few preliminary experiments when his work was interrupted by World War I. Hostilities had been raging in Europe since 1914 but now, on April 6, 1917, the United States entered the war. A few days later, Goddard wrote to the Smithsonian suggesting military uses for rockets and offering his services. The U.S. Army Signal Corps, acting on a recommendation by the Smithsonian, asked Goddard to develop rockets that would be useful in battle.

After a few months of preliminary work in Worcester, Goddard was asked to move his laboratory to the famous observatory at Mount Wilson in Pasadena, California. The rocket project was top secret, and there were indications that spies were attempting to gain access to his lab in Worcester. Accordingly, Goddard's equipment was shipped by rail in innocent-looking crates. The explosives he would need were packed into suitcases that Goddard himself carried on the long train journey to California. Once there, Goddard developed prototypes for several kinds of solid propellant rockets designed especially for military uses.

On November 7, 1918, Goddard demonstrated the rockets at the Aberdeen Proving Ground in Maryland for a group of repre-

Robert H. Goddard invented the forerunner of the bazooka. This 1918 photo shows him loading the bazooka tube with a projectile. (Goddard Collection/Clark University)

sentatives from the U.S. Army, Navy, and Air Service. One of the rockets was a long-range bombardment rocket which, unlike an artillery shell, required no cannon to launch it. Another was a rocket that could be fired from a light-weight recoilless launcher that an ordinary soldier could hold in his hands or balance on his shoulder. Although it had very little "kick" for the soldier who fired it, the launcher was designed to fire a penetrating charge that had the power to stop tanks. This forerunner of the modern bazooka impressed the military men very much, and they were anxious to put it, as well as some of the other rockets, into production for use in actual combat. Four days later, however, the war ended with the Armistice, and the plans to produce Bob Goddard's war rockets were put on a shelf, where they gathered dust for more than 20 years.

CHAPTER 3 NOTES

p. 26   "The most wonderful thing . . ." PRHG, Vol. I, p. 104.

p. 26   "See it through . . ." PRHG, Vol. I, p. 105.

p. 26   "You did yourself proud . . ." PRHG, Vol. I, p. 106.

p. 29   "Shall I ever be able . . ." PRHG, Vol. I, p. 18.

p. 29   "they give as nearly as possible . . ." PRHG, Vol. I, p. 19.

p. 32   "It went!" PRHG, Vol. I, p. 161.

p. 33   "The class yelled . . ." PRHG, Vol. I, p. 167.

p. 34   "Dreamed . . . of going to the moon . . ." PRHG, Vol. I, p. 163.

p. 34   "It was almost impossible . . ." Shelley M. Lauzon, *Robert Hutchings Goddard Memorial Dedication* (pamphlet), p. 8.

p. 35   "a method of raising . . ." PRHG, Vol. I, p. 170.

p. 35   "We are greatly interested . . ." PRHG, Vol. I, p. 176.

p. 35   "I do not think that the work . . ." PRHG, Vol. I, p. 178.

p. 36   "Read letter to Ma and Pa . . ." PRHG, Vol. I, p. 191.

4

MOON MAN

"Every vision is a joke until the first man accomplishes it. Once realized, it becomes commonplace."
—Dr. Robert H. Goddard

With the signing of the Armistice on November 11, 1918, World War I, the "war to end all wars," was finally over. Bob Goddard, like people everywhere, looked forward to returning to normal life. His work in California had been absorbing and exciting, but underneath it all he had felt an aching homesickness. Before the end of 1918, he was back again in Worcester, happy to be reunited with his family and eager to resume his work in the laboratories at Clark University. He was particularly interested in exploring the idea of using liquid propellants in rockets, and began laying plans to put his theories to the test. Shortly after he returned to Clark, however, an unsettling incident occurred.

On March 28, 1919, the *Worcester Evening Gazette* printed an item picked up from the Associated Press, a news service that sends stories to newspapers throughout the country. The headline read, INVENTS ROCKET WITH ALTITUDE RANGE OF 70 MILES, and the story related how a "terrible engine of war" had been invented by Dr. Robert H. Goddard under the patronage of the U.S. War Department. In Washington, D.C., the *Washington Star* carried a similar lengthy article about Goddard's secret work for the military. Someone, probably one of the officials who had been present at the Aberdeen tests, had leaked top secret information to the press. The story created a mild sensation and, suddenly, all kinds of people were interested in Goddard's work.

Robert H. Goddard used this circular vacuum tube in experiments proving that rockets operate more efficiently in a vacuum than in air. This photo was included in his book, *A Method of Reaching Extreme Altitudes.*
(Goddard Collection/Clark University)

Now that some of Goddard's activities had been made public, Dr. Arthur G. Webster, director of the Physical Laboratories at Clark, urged him to publish information on his rocket work, going so far as to say that if Goddard didn't do so, he would do so himself. To prevent this from happening, Goddard wrote to the Smithsonian to ask if they would be willing to publish a manuscript he had sent to them a few years earlier. Dr. C. G. Abbot replied promptly, saying that, yes, the Smithsonian would publish the paper but that the cost of its publication would be deducted from Goddard's research funds.

Goddard set to work immediately updating the manuscript to include his latest research. In January 1920, the Smithsonian published *A Method of Reaching Extreme Altitudes*, a remarkable treatise on the basics of rocketry that is now considered one of the fundamental classics of space science. In it, Goddard explained the mathematics of rockets; described the results of his early experiments; discussed the concept of step, or multistage, rockets; and included computations that showed that a rocket equipped with an efficient engine and appropriate propellants could travel to great heights. He added notes about his recent experiments, the possible use of hydrogen and oxygen as fuels, and the probability of collision with meteors. Goddard had written the treatise for his fellow scientists and, with sections carrying such titles as "Reduction of Equation to the Simplest Form" and "Calculations Based on Theory and Experiment," it seemed unlikely that anyone beyond a small group of scholars would ever read it.

The last section of the book was titled "Calculation of Minimum Mass Required to Raise One Pound to an 'Infinite' Altitude." In it, Goddard speculated, almost as an afterthought, that it would one day be possible to send a rocket to the moon. To prove that such an extreme altitude had been attained, he suggested that the rocket carry a pound or two of photographic flash powder that would explode on impact with the moon's surface. If the rocket were to land on the dark surface of the moon, he wrote, the ignited flash powder would be visible through a powerful telescope. But, he added, "this plan of sending a mass of flash powder to the surface of the moon, although a matter of much general interest, is not of obvious scientific importance. There are, however, developments of the general method under discussion, which involve a number of important features not herein mentioned, which could lead to results of much scientific interest. These developments involve many experimental difficulties, to be sure; but they depend upon nothing that is really impossible."

Only 1,750 copies of the small, slender book were printed. Upon publication, it was sent free of charge to libraries and universities across the country. A press release announcing the book's publication was sent by the Smithsonian to various scientific journals. In Worcester, Goddard modestly accepted congratulations from his family and colleagues. He had no idea that his life was about to change.

On January 12, 1920, Goddard got the first indication that something was wrong. When he opened the pages of the *Boston Herald*, a headline leaped out at him: NEW ROCKET DEVISED BY PROF. GODDARD MAY HIT FACE OF MOON. Although mildly annoyed by the unwarranted publicity, he was willing to dismiss the story as an example of silly journalism. Nothing, however, could have prepared him for what happened next.

It seemed that a copy of the Smithsonian's press release had fallen into the hands of a newspaper reporter whose sharp eyes landed on the words *infinite altitude*. Wasn't that just another way of saying "space flight"? Today, it is difficult to realize how crazy and ridiculous the idea of space flight appeared to people in the 1920s. Even scientists and engineers at that time ridiculed the notion as utterly fantastic, and labeled anyone who took it seriously a crackpot. It is not surprising, therefore, that the reporter seized on Goddard's "moon rocket" idea to write a sensational story about the crazy scientist who wanted to shoot at the moon.

Suddenly, everybody wanted to know about Robert Goddard. Newspapers across the country jumped on the story, referring to him derisively as the "Moon Man" and challenging his scientific knowledge. MODERN JULES VERNE INVENTS ROCKET TO GO TO MOON, proclaimed a headline in the *Boston American*. And a reporter for The *New York Times* remarked disdainfully that Goddard "only seems to lack the knowledge ladled out daily in high schools." Hardly anyone, it seemed, paid attention to his mathematics, experiments, and technical achievements. Instead, he was accused of deliberately distorting scientific facts to suit his purposes.

Goddard responded by sending a statement to the Associated Press in which he tried to direct public attention away from the moon rocket idea to the less-sensational portions of his book. Although it was printed in some newspapers, his statement had little effect.

In response to the more serious charges of fellow scientists who questioned his theories and the integrity of his experiments, Goddard submitted a report to the Smithsonian Institution in March 1920. The report, titled "Concerning Further Developments of the Rocket Method of Investigating Space," outlined how rockets, powered by liquid oxygen and hydrogen, could be sent to distant planets. Filled with visionary ideas that were nevertheless based on solid research and logical theory, the report discussed such topics as the control of unmanned space vehicles, manned space flights, ion propulsion, and a method for harnessing the sun's energy for propulsion in space. Goddard even suggested that contact might be made with inhabitants of other planets by sending "devices containing metal sheets stamped with geometrical figures, with the constellations (emphasizing the earth and moon), together with as much description as possible of the rocket itself." Years later, plates such as these were, in fact, placed aboard a deep-space probe when NASA launched *Pioneer 10* in 1972.

Still, despite his efforts, few people seemed to listen to Goddard. Overnight, his life had turned into a nightmare. Droves of reporters descended on Worcester to pound on his door and seek an interview with the "mad scientist." He was polite to everyone, but he courteously declined to grant any interviews. His silence, however, managed only to stimulate the public's curiosity and to provoke even more speculation about him and his projects.

A new wave of wild stories about the "Mystery Professor" appeared, their writers purporting to describe his clandestine preparations for a journey to the moon. To add to Goddard's distress and embarrassment, cartoons poking fun at him appeared on the editorial pages of newspapers across the country. Moon-rocket jokes, which seemed to pop up from nowhere, swept the nation.

Everyone in America, it seemed, knew about the "crazy" professor in Massachusetts. Every day, Goddard's mailbox was stuffed with letters. Many people wrote volunteering to ride as passengers on the moon rocket. One man expressed his concern that a flight to the moon might anger the lunar inhabitants and provoke them to "arrange some method of destroying or injuring the earth." A New York entrepreneur, eager to cash in on the moon mania, wrote, "As undoubtedly you will desire some special starting point from which to start this rocket, and one at which the greatest number of people could have the opportunity to observe its departure, the Bronx Exposition, Inc. offers the use of Starlight Amusement Park for the purpose, and at the same time will be happy to provide all the facilities needed for the occasion."

Had he been able to foresee the sensation that his theories would create, Goddard would have eliminated all mention of moon rockets from his treatise. "In trying to minimize the sensational side," he wrote, "I had really made more of a stir than if I had discussed transportation to Mars, which would probably have been considered ridiculous . . . and doubtless never mentioned."

The effect of all this publicity on the shy, sensitive physicist was to make him even more wary about discussing his work openly and more reticent about granting interviews. For the remainder of his life, Goddard shunned publicity of any kind. He had learned a hard lesson: that being a pioneer, especially the pioneer of a bold, new idea, can be a painful, lonely experience. Many years later, in 1945, he was to write, "The subject of projection from the earth, and especially a mention of the moon, must still be avoided in dignified scientific and engineering circles."

Although few people in America took Goddard's report seriously, the reaction in Europe was different. The idea that the rocket was the key to space travel had already dawned on several European researchers.

One of these men, a Russian scientist-schoolteacher named Konstantin Eduardovitch Tsiolkovsky, had grasped the reaction principle underlying rocket motion as early as 1883, when Bob Goddard was only one year old. But working alone, with meager equipment and scanty funds, Tsiolkovsky had been unable to confirm his theories with actual experiments. By 1919, however, he had worked out the theoretical aspects of rocket propulsion and interplanetary flight, describing in his writings both the multistage rocket and the use of liquid hydrogen and liquid oxygen as fuels.

With little support or recognition from the government of the U.S.S.R., Tsiolkovsky continued his theoretical investigations until his death in 1935, without ever having put his brilliant theories to the test. It remained to Robert Goddard to combine theory with practice in an extraordinary career that was to earn him the well-deserved title of "Father of Modern Rocketry."

Tsiolkovsky almost certainly never saw Bob Goddard's book, but when articles about *A Method of Reaching Extreme Altitudes* appeared in foreign newspapers, the work attracted the attention of several other European scientists. One of them was a French airplane designer and manufacturer named Robert Esnault-Pelterie. He wrote to Goddard saying that he himself had already published a paper showing that radioactive energy was the only practical way to power interplanetary flights. Goddard sent a copy of his own book to Esnault-Pelterie, pointing out his discussion of both solid and liquid propellants, as well as his explanation of the multistage rocket principle whereby empty casings were discarded so that a large, constant ratio of propellant to casing (or rocket) could be maintained. Years later, in 1930, Esnault-Pelterie published a book incorporating many of Goddard's ideas.

Another scientist who read newspaper accounts of Goddard's work was Hermann Oberth, a Hungarian-born German physicist, who was later acknowledged as one of the great pioneers of rocketry and astronautics. Unable to obtain *A Method of Reaching Extreme Altitudes* in Germany, Oberth wrote to Goddard in 1922. In requesting a copy of the book, he explained that "already many years I work at the problem to pass over the atmosphere of our earth by means of a rocket," and added, "I think that only by the common work of scholars of all nations can be solved this great problem."

Unlike his German counterpart, Goddard preferred to work alone, but he promptly sent a copy of the book to Oberth. In 1923, Hermann Oberth published his own book, *Die Rakete zu den Planetenräumen* (*The Rocket into Planetary Space*), in which he included a discussion comparing Goddard's work with his own. Although he claimed that he had worked independently, Oberth's conclusions closely resembled Goddard's. Upon reading Oberth's book, Goddard was upset by the resemblances to his own work. He quickly wrote a letter to the Smithsonian presenting an update of his most recent rocket experiments and adding this prophetic comment: "I am not surprised that Germany has awakened to the importance and the development possibilities of the work, and I would not be surprised if it were only a matter of time before the research would become something in the nature of a race."

Oberth later became Germany's foremost rocket expert, numbering among his students and followers such scientists as Wernher von Braun and Willy Ley. Throughout his life, however, Oberth was haunted by the notion that people might think he owed his ideas to Goddard and that they might accuse him of having copied Goddard's work. His concern was not without substance. Years later, during World War II, Oberth and others lent their scientific talents to the German war machine. The German V-2 rockets they developed—the rockets that devastated London—bore a marked resemblance to Goddard's original rocket design.

Being the butt of jokes and the target of ridicule was not easy for the shy, dignified scientist. It is not surprising, therefore, that Goddard was especially pleased when a few of his own countrymen expressed serious interest in the substance of his work. One of them was the great inventor Alexander Graham Bell. Excited by the possibility of using rockets to power a hydrofoil boat that he was in the process of developing, Bell paid Goddard's travel expenses to Washington, D.C., so that he could discuss the project with the young physicist. Bell was impressed by Goddard's ideas, while Goddard found that Dr. Bell, "an old man at the time, was keen-minded and of very pleasing manner."

The government, too, took an interest in Goddard's work. The Weather Bureau wanted to explore the idea of using rockets to collect high-altitude data that would make weather forecasting more accurate and reliable. The military continued to be interested in Goddard's ideas, as well. Although the urgency to develop new weapons had ended with the Armistice, a limited amount of weapons research was still being conducted. Goddard was invited to develop an antisubmarine rocket device for the U.S. Navy and, at the same time, the U.S. Army's Chemical Warfare Service approached him about the possibility of developing rockets to carry gas, incendiaries, and high explosives. At home in Worcester, the trustees at Clark University demonstrated their support of

Goddard by voting to advance him to a full professorship "as an appreciation of [his] valuable scientific work."

It was gratifying to know that not everyone thought he was a crackpot. Still, considering the furor created by the mere mention of a flight to the moon, Goddard was privately grateful that no one knew about the extreme speculations he had included in a manuscript written in 1918, a time when the horrors of World War I made the future of the world seem uncertain. Entitled "The Last Migration," the paper considered the possibility that someday people would have to send expeditions to distant planets in order to preserve the human race. It described how spaceships, fueled either by atomic energy or by a combination of hydrogen, oxygen, and solar energy, would travel to the distant reaches of space, carrying people in suspended animation.

After writing the paper, Goddard had sealed it in an envelope, enclosed it in a second envelope which he labeled "Special Formulae for Silvering Mirrors," and then deposited it in a friend's safe. This extraordinary document can now be seen at the Goddard Library at Clark University.

Despite all the commotion that the publication of his book had caused, Goddard's thoughts never strayed very far from his work. He had resumed full-time teaching at Clark, where he continued to delight and inspire his students. For the "hams" and radio enthusiasts in his classes, he organized and guided the Wireless Club, which later made the first radio broadcasts heard in Worcester. Once again, his days were devoted to teaching. He had only spare time to devote to his research, but he was ready to begin a new phase of rocket development.

Before Goddard could begin, however, fate struck yet another blow. His mother, who had suffered from tuberculosis for many years, finally succumbed to the disease. Never one to engage in showy displays of emotion, Goddard noted her passing in his diary with these simple words: "Mother died at 1:35." After Fannie Goddard's funeral, father and son returned with heavy hearts to the home the three of them had shared. Upstairs in the smoking room, the two men talked quietly, sharing their grief and trying to imagine what life would be like without Fannie's sunny, supportive presence. Neither man, however, railed against the gods. With typical New England stoicism, they accepted the tragedy of their loss and vowed to get on with their lives.

It was an attitude that Bob Goddard maintained throughout his life. Whenever he was faced with setbacks and adversities, he would calmly pick up the pieces and go on. He never wasted time on anger or regrets. "It's appalling how short life is, and how much there is to do one would like to do," he had written back in 1915. "We have to be sports, take chances, and do what we can."

For the most part, 1920 had been a terrible year for Bob Goddard in both his public and private life. Perhaps that is why his annual Anniversary Day pilgrimage to the cherry tree behind his grandmother's barn lasted longer than usual. Caught in the spell of the quiet October afternoon, he leaned back against the trunk of the tree, munching apples and gazing at the familiar, autumn-tinted hills beyond. Time passed, but still he lingered. He seemed to draw a spiritual sustenance through the rough bark of the tree and, as he reflected on all that had happened, the memory of his youthful vision once again shone brightly in his mind's eye. He felt a strengthening of resolve, a renewal of his dream to one day send humans beyond the stars. It did not matter what other people said or thought about him—nothing mattered—nothing but the vision and the dream.

CHAPTER 4 NOTES

p. 39   "Every vision is a joke . . ." Shelley M. Lauzon, *Robert Hutchings Goddard Memorial Dedication* (pamphlet), p. 10.

pp. 41–42   "this plan of sending . . ." Robert H. Goddard, *A Method of Reaching Extreme Altitudes.* Included in PRHG, Vol. I, p. 395.

p. 42   "only seems to lack . . ." Shelley M. Lauzon, *Robert Hutchings Goddard Memorial Dedication* (pamphlet), p. 10.

p. 43   "devices containing metal sheets . . ." PRHG, Vol. I, p. 416.

p. 44   "arrange some method of destroying . . ." PRHG, Vol. I, p. 411.

p. 44   "As undoubtedly you will desire . . ." PRHG, Vol. I, p. 409.

p. 44   "In trying to minimize . . ." PRHG, Vol. I, p. 24.

p. 44   "The subject of projection . . ." PRHG, Vol. I, p. 1596.

p. 45   "already many years I work . . ." PRHG, Vol. I, p. 485.

p. 46   "I am not surprised . . ." PRHG, Vol. I, p. 498.

p. 46   "an old man at the time . . ." PRHG, Vol. I, p. 28.

p. 47   "as an appreciation of . . ." PRHG, Vol. I, p. 446.

p. 47   "Mother died at 1:35." PRHG, Vol. I, p. 412.

p. 48   "It's appalling how short . . ." PRHG, Vol. I, p. 157.

5

LOX AND LOVE

"Experience enables one to apply things that one knows; theoretical science enables one to apply things that have never been dreamed of."
—Dr. Robert H. Goddard

"The bride wore a gown of white . . . and a corsage bouquet."
—Worcester Evening Post

Although the publication of his book resulted in public embarrassment, and the death of his mother caused him personal sorrow, the biggest problems facing Robert Goddard in 1920 had to do with a shortage of money and a plague of troubles in the laboratory.

For several years, Goddard had focused his efforts on developing solid fuel rockets that used several varieties of gunpowder as fuel. The more he experimented, however, the more difficulties he encountered. The use of black powder, nitrocellulose smokeless powder, and other solid fuels posed several thorny problems that were hard to overcome.

Goddard's experiments demonstrated that, in order to operate a solid fuel rocket successfully, the fuel had to be fed gradually into the combustion chamber, where it was then fired. To accomplish this, he had invented a mechanism that operated on the same principle as a magazine, which automatically fires cartridges into the chamber of a gun. Then, in order to prevent burning particles from escaping the combustion chamber and causing the powder in the reserve fuel chambers to explode, he had devised yet another mechanism. Although the mechanisms worked effectively, they added weight to the rocket. The heavier a rocket is, the more power is necessary to obtain "lift." Adding more fuel was not the answer; it would only increase the weight of the rocket, which would then need even more power to lift it. To provide the needed power, Goddard reasoned that he would have to increase the efficiency of the fuel and to increase the velocity at which the gases were ejected, while keeping the weight of the rocket itself at a minimum.

To overcome these problems, Goddard devised several ingenious refinements of the fuel-feeding mechanisms and, by narrowing and lengthening the exhaust nozzle, he was able to increase the force of the ejected gases. The result was an increase in the velocity of an ordinary rocket from 1,000 feet per second to 8,000 feet per second. By gradually streamlining and modifying his designs, he had managed to produce efficient, effective solid-fuel rockets capable of short, horizontal flights such as those attained by the bazooka rocket, which he had pioneered for the U.S. Army.

After many experiments, however, Goddard concluded that, while solid fuels could be used successfully with small rockets, they were unreliable in lifting larger rockets and keeping them in flight. The biggest obstacle lay in the way the powder was packed into the rocket. If it was packed too tightly, it burned slowly and did not generate enough force to lift the rocket. Packing it too loosely, however, could cause a sudden explosion that would destroy the rocket and seriously threaten anyone nearby. How to keep a large rocket on a steady path once it had been launched posed yet another problem. Too often, his experiments resulted in frustrating failure. Sometimes the combustion chambers exploded, sometimes the fuel-feeding mechanisms failed, and sometimes the stabilizers did not stabilize. Solid fuel rockets required too many complicated mechanisms; too much could go wrong.

Although he had been able to solve many of the difficulties posed by the use of solid fuels, Goddard became convinced that his rockets would never reach high altitudes if he continued to use solid fuels as propellants. The time had come, he decided, to begin experimenting with liquid fuels, an idea that had first occurred to him as early as 1909.

The advantage of a liquid-fuel rocket was that the fuel tank and the combustion mechanism could be very simple and, therefore, light in weight. The disadvantage lay in the fact that such liquids as hydrogen, oxygen, nitrous oxide, and ether are highly explosive, treacherous materials. Working with them could be extremely hazardous. Fully aware of the dangers involved, Goddard was determined nevertheless to begin working with liquid fuels. If his rockets were ever to reach extreme altitudes, he would have to find a way to tame and control these volatile liquids.

There was no doubt in Goddard's mind that liquid-fuel rockets would one day be capable of sending people to the moon and beyond. His calculations had already proved that the idea was theoretically possible. It remained only to confirm the theory with practical experiments. He decided that the most promising liquid fuel would be a combination of liquid oxygen (called "lox") and gasoline. His head was filled with ideas, his heart was filled with enthusiasm, and his fingers itched to begin. The only thing he lacked was money.

When the U.S. Navy Bureau of Ordnance offered him a $100-a-month grant to develop an antisubmarine rocket device, Goddard accepted. From July 1920 until March 1923, Goddard spent his weekends and vacation time working for the navy at Indian Head, Maryland, where he developed plans for a depth-charge rocket as well as a rocket that could carry an armor-piercing warhead.

In addition to his work for the navy, Goddard, now a full professor of physics, taught a crowded schedule of classes at Clark University. Considering that he was also trying to conduct research in his spare time, as well as traveling back and forth to Maryland on weekends, it would be understandable if Goddard had devoted only minimal time to his students. But that was not the case. A dedicated and inspiring teacher, Goddard always made time for students who needed his help.

One of Goddard's students remembered him this way: "I was very fortunate when, as a senior . . . I registered to take one of Goddard's advanced courses. He and I soon learned that I was the only student who had signed for that course . . . Would New York University, where I later taught for forty years, allow a professor to give a course for *one* student? No! No! . . . But at Clark it was all right. . . . We met in his office at stated intervals, where he quizzed me and gave me problems to work out. It was not only a good learning situation, but it gave me a fine opportunity to get to know him. . . . Dr. Robert Hutchings Goddard was one of the finest men I have known during my life of eighty-eight years."

For all his dedication, Goddard was paid an annual salary of $2,000 by Clark. This sum, added to the money he was receiving from the navy, provided him with an income of more than $3,000 a year—sufficient to provide an ordinary person with a comfortable existence at that time, but not nearly enough for a scientist engaged in costly experimentation.

In 1916, Goddard had been awarded a $5,000 grant for rocket research by the Smithsonian Institution. He had made careful use of every dollar, but now, in 1920, the funds were running out. With little more than $1,000 left in the grant fund, Goddard knew that he would have to find more money if his research were to continue. Hoping to have the grant renewed, Goddard sent a description of his proposed experiments to the Smithsonian, stressing, as always, the practical uses to which rockets could be put. "Unfortunately," the reply read, "owing to the pressure of other requirements the Institution is quite unable to make further grants at this time, although it would be desirous to do so if the money were available."

Next, Goddard approached the U.S. Weather Bureau with the idea of developing rockets to gather meteorological data for the purpose of weather forecasting. The officials appointed to assess Goddard's proposal reported that, while they recognized the importance and desirability of the project, there were simply no funds available to underwrite the research.

Undaunted, Goddard directed his next appeal closer to home. In a letter to the trustees of Clark University, he asked for a grant of $5,000 "for the completion of a preliminary model of a multiple-charge rocket to be used in high-altitude investigations." This time he met with success.

In June 1921, Goddard was delighted to receive word that the Clark trustees were awarding him $2,500 for his work. This sum, together with an additional grant of $1,000 in 1922, made it possible for Goddard to continue tests with solid fuel multiple-charge rockets. More important, it allowed him to begin the work he was most anxious to do—experiments with liquid-fuel rockets.

Although he did not have nearly enough money to cover the experiments he had in mind, Goddard looked confidently to the future. He was sure that if he stretched every penny to the utmost, somehow, someday, he would succeed.

Goddard's first experiments with lox (liquid oxygen) were dismal failures. But *failure* was not, and never would be, a word in his vocabulary. Methodically, he recorded the results in his notebooks, carefully preserving the "valuable negative information" the experiments had yielded, and vowing to try and try again.

Life had dealt him some nasty blows, he was overworked and very tired, and the results in his laboratory were disappointing— but nothing seemed to dampen his buoyant spirits. Gradually, surprisingly, a special kind of happiness had crept into his life. Robert Goddard was in love.

Back in 1919, when Robert Goddard was 37 years old, he appeared to be an unlikely candidate for romance. He was a tall, thin, mustachioed man with warm brown eyes and a nearly bald

Goddard at the blackboard at Clark University, explaining how a rocket might reach the moon. (Goddard Collection/Clark University)

head. People who knew him were attracted by his shy, modest manner, his lively intelligence, and his gentle personality. They admired his dedication and perseverance, but they wondered how he could find time for ordinary social activities if he spent all his time working. If he continued to bury himself in a classroom or laboratory, how could he ever meet someone and start a family of his own? Since he gave no indication that he would ever change his habits, everyone concluded that Bob Goddard was destined to remain a bachelor.

In October of that year, when Goddard finished writing the book that was to bring him so much attention, he decided to have the manuscript professionally typed before sending it off to the Smithsonian Institution. Someone suggested that he offer the job to Esther Kisk, the young woman who had recently been hired as secretary to Edmund C. Sanford, the president of Clark. Accordingly, on October 9, he set off for the president's office with his manuscript under his arm.

There is no record of the words that passed between the shy professor and the pretty young woman, but that night Goddard wrote in his diary, "Went to Miss Kisk's with MS," adding, with a hint at the romantic feelings that may have been stirring inside him, that he "played piano in evening." His diary records that a few weeks later he washed and polished his car, and took Miss Kisk on an afternoon outing to Leicester and Charlton.

Only something or someone important could have compelled Goddard to put aside his work in order to spend the day driving through the countryside. He may not have realized at the time how central a role Miss Kisk was to play in his life, but he knew that a certain chemistry had been born between them and that a law of nature—not one of Newton's laws this time—had been set in motion.

With a 20-year age difference between them, Robert Goddard and Esther Christine Kisk seemed an unlikely couple at first. Only 17 years old at the time, Kisk was a tall, attractive blonde girl with a keen intelligence and sparkling wit. She lived at home with her parents and was working in order to save enough money to pay for her college tuition. To earn extra money, she typed manuscripts and theses in her spare time. Like Goddard, Kisk was reserved and determined, and it was not long before the two of them discovered many common interests. They shared a love of music and art, and they began attending concerts and visiting museums together whenever time allowed. Their closeness grew when Goddard discovered that Kisk was interested in science as well.

Despite his busy schedule, Goddard paid regular visits to Kisk. In a letter to the author, a former student recalled that, while he was attending Clark, "a beautiful young lady who was [the president's] secretary lived next door with her parents. Very often in the evenings I used to see Dr. Goddard's coupé parked in front of her house. Those were his courting days."

As the weeks and months passed, their relationship grew stronger. While the world outside was busy making fun of the "moon man" and his "crazy" rocket ideas, Kisk's respect and adoration for the gentle scientist blossomed into love. For his part, Goddard came to the gradual realization that, with Kisk at his side, even his wildest dreams might someday become reality. In the spring of 1922, he asked Esther Kisk to become his wife. The *Worcester Telegram* broadcast the news of their engagement under a headline that read PROFESSOR AND STUDENT TO WED.

By this time, Kisk had managed to save enough money to attend Bates College in Lewiston, Maine. Accustomed to her smiling, happy ways and to the enjoyment she brought to everything and everybody, Goddard missed her very much. He sent a steady stream of letters and fancy boxes of candy to his "golden girl." He told her about his research and experiments, about his plans and hopes and dreams.

Kisk, caught up in Goddard's enthusiasm, decided that her proper place was by his side. She left college and, on June 21, 1924, Esther Kisk and Robert Goddard were married in a simple ceremony in St. John's Episcopal Church. There were no attendants, no large reception; only Esther's parents, Nahum Goddard (along with his second wife, whom he had married in 1921), and a few friends were on hand to celebrate the occasion. But Robert and Esther Goddard needed no great fanfare to validate their marriage; they shared a deep love that was to endure for the rest of their lives.

After the wedding, the newlyweds set off in Goddard's coupé for a honeymoon trip through the White Mountains of New Hamp-

Goddard and rocket with double-acting engine, November 1925. After two years of experiments using separate pumps for each propellant, Goddard decided to combine both pumps into a single double-acting unit. This idea marked a significant advance toward a successful solution of the pump problem. (Goddard Collection/Clark University)

shire. When they returned to Worcester a few weeks later, they made their home at 1 Tallawanda Drive. Once known as Maple Hill, it was the same house that had belonged to Goddard's grandmother—the house behind which stood Goddard's beloved cherry tree.

Goddard, who had always worked alone, found in Esther not only a cherished wife but a valuable partner. For several years, he had relied on her to type his papers. Now she also became his "official" photographer, bookkeeper, and laboratory assistant. Well versed in scientific language, she carefully organized his notes and papers—documents that later proved to be a valuable record of her husband's life work.

Money was always in short supply in the Goddard household, but Esther found a thousand ways to economize so that every stray nickel could be spent on the equipment and supplies Goddard needed for his experiments. She saved up enough to buy a motion picture camera so that she would be able to photograph his rocket launchings. And she helped him build equipment from anything the two of them could beg or borrow. When Goddard needed a rocket-launching frame, he and Esther bought a farm windmill through the Sears, Roebuck catalog. As soon as the windmill was delivered, the Goddards set to work converting it to its new use. After learning that a chemical company was throwing away liquid oxygen, the Goddards arranged to buy it cheaply and haul it away themselves.

For many long months, Goddard spend his evenings and weekends developing a liquid-fuel rocket motor, using lox and gasoline as propellants. Finally, in December 1925, Goddard had something wonderful to report to Esther. In his small laboratory at Clark, he tested his latest lightweight motor. At first it shuddered in its stand; then, for 24 exciting seconds, the motor lifted itself from its moorings. The lox and gasoline mixture was doing what he had meant it to do. The next step, he told Esther, was flight.

CHAPTER 5 NOTES

p. 50   "Experience enables one . . ." PRHG, Vol. I, p. 76.

p. 50   "The bride wore a gown . . ." PRHG, Vol. I, p. 545.

pp. 52–53   "I was very fortunate when . . ." Letter from Dr. Ralph W. Gilbert of Sturbridge, Massachusetts, to the author.

p. 53   "Unfortunately, owing to the pressure . . ." PRHG, Vol. I, p. 471.

p. 53   "for the completion of . . ." PRHG, Vol. I, p. 469.

p. 55   "Went to Miss Kisk's . . ." PRHG, Vol. I, p. 337.

p. 56   "a beautiful young lady . . ." Letter from Dr. Ralph W. Gilbert of Sturbridge, Massachusetts, to the author.

p. 56   "Professor and student . . ." PRHG, Vol. I, p. 483.

6

TWO-AND-A-HALF SECONDS TO HISTORY

"It looked almost magical as it rose . . ."
—Dr. Robert H. Goddard

After more than two years of working on the design for a liquid-fuel rocket motor, Robert Goddard was ready to build a rocket for flight testing. His earlier rockets had been made from brass, but now, in an attempt to reduce weight to a minimum, he decided to use magnesium and aluminum alloys for some of the parts. For other parts he used a special kind of English sheet steel because it proved to be much stronger than domestic steel. At a local hardware store, he found nuts, bolts, steel piping, and other standard items he needed. He purchased all of these materials with his own money and hired a machinist to manufacture special parts for the rocket, paying for the man's services with small sums that he received from the Smithsonian Institution.

Because of the expense involved, Goddard made his rocket as small as possible. "It is the same old story of no support until results are had, and no results unless sufficient support is had," he wrote an acquaintance. "It would be much more exciting to work on a larger scale, but it is not possible to think of that now." He had to make do with what he had and hope that the Smithsonian would grant him more funds when he had proved that he could send a liquid-fuel rocket into actual flight.

Several years earlier, after people complained of the roars and explosions coming from the neighborhood of the Clark physics building, Goddard had begun conducting his noisier tests on a farm in Auburn owned by Miss Effie Ward, a distant relative. "Aunt" Effie, who raised strawberries with the help of a hired man, allowed Goddard to set up a testing tower in a back pasture and offered him a vacant henhouse to store his equipment. She was proud of her eccentric kinsman, and whenever an occasional explosion rocked the farm, she took it in stride and asked no questions.

Early on the morning of Tuesday, March 16, 1926, Goddard met his machinist, Henry Sachs, at the Clark physics building. Goddard, who had been appointed chairman of the physics department several years before, had no classes scheduled for that day. After loading the new test rocket and other equipment onto a trailer attached to the car, the two men climbed into Goddard's coupé. Goddard preferred driving a coupé (a two-seat car) because, he explained, "you don't have to take an excess of people." On the seat between them sat two liters of liquid oxygen. Not only was "lox" expensive (each liter cost 10 dollars), it was difficult to obtain. If today's test failed, it might be a month or longer before he would be able to obtain more liquid oxygen for another test.

The air was cold and sharp, and the ground was covered with a thin blanket of snow as Goddard drove carefully along the slippery roads to Aunt Effie's farm. Esther Goddard, always concerned about her husband's health, had insisted that he dress warmly. He sat at the steering wheel, bundled up in a long coat, a muffler, a woolen cap, galoshes, and gloves.

At last they reached the Ward farm. After parking some distance from the farmhouse, Goddard and Sachs unloaded the wooden crates containing tools, the rocket motor, pipes, and tanks. They half-carried, half-slid the crates to an out-of-the-way spot near a cabbage patch, where they spent the morning erecting a launching frame out of pipes. When the frame was ready, they positioned the rocket in place.

The rocket itself consisted of a motor and nozzle measuring two feet in length, framed by tubing that brought its total height to about 10 feet. It had no outer covering as modern rockets do. In appearance the rocket was small and fragile, but it represented the culmination of years of experimentation.

Main Features of Goddard's 1926 Liquid–Fuel Rocket

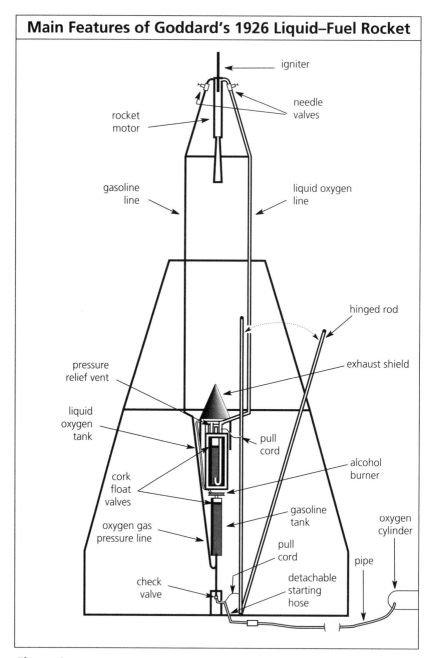

Figure 2

In designing his first liquid-fuel rocket, Goddard had to overcome many obstacles. A liquid fuel needs a steady source of oxygen in order to burn at a rate that will produce the desired rocket thrust. After many experiments, he had chosen gasoline as the fuel and liquid oxygen as the oxidizer.

Next, Goddard had developed a method for combining the fuel and the oxidizer at the proper rate in the combustion chamber. He did this by taking advantage of the special properties of oxygen. When it is very cold, at temperatures of -297°F and below, oxygen is a liquid. When a container of liquid oxygen is warmed, the lox turns into a gas and produces tremendous pressures inside the container. Goddard's rocket harnessed this pressure to force both liquids from their tanks at the same time, sending the lox and the gasoline through separate pipes to the combustion chamber, where they combined and burned. To hasten the vaporizing of the lox, Goddard would apply heat from an alcohol burner to the container of liquid oxygen.

Altogether, the rocket was a masterpiece of mechanical ingenuity. A pipe for the pressurizing gas ran between the gasoline tank and the lox tank. If the liquids were to pass through this pipe and mix with each other before reaching the combustion chamber, an explosion would occur. To prevent this from happening, Goddard used cork floats that would keep the liquid from sloshing into the pipe but would still allow gas to flow through. The gas pressure would be the only means for pumping the gasoline and lox once the rocket was launched.

Before the rocket left the ground, however, another means of pressurizing the system would be needed. To accomplish this, Goddard placed a cylinder containing oxygen about 30 feet from the rocket. He used a heavy rubber hose to connect the cylinder to the rocket's pressure line. When the rocket began to rise, he would pull the hose free. A check valve would then immediately slam shut over the connective opening to prevent any loss of pressure.

It was a few minutes past noon when Goddard and Sachs finished checking their work. They looked with satisfaction at the rocket gleaming in the cold winter sunshine as it stood ready on its launching frame. Several feet away stood a sheet-iron barricade that would give them protection when the rocket was launched.

At one o'clock Esther Goddard arrived, accompanied by Percy Roope, an assistant professor of physics as Clark. Slung over her shoulder was a brand new spring-operated motion picture camera, guaranteed to run for seven seconds without rewinding. Aunt Effie appeared with a hospitable offer of hot malted milk for the group gathered in her pasture.

By 2:30, Goddard and his helpers were finally ready for the countdown. First, Henry Sachs, using a blowtorch fastened to a long pole, heated the igniter casing. The igniter contained some match heads and black powder. When the casing became hot, the match heads burst into flame and ignited the black powder, which sent out a cloud of black smoke. Sachs then quickly

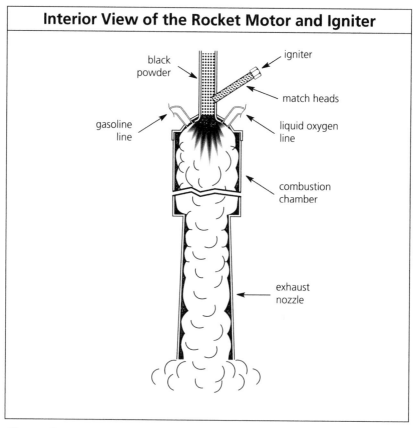

Interior View of the Rocket Motor and Igniter

black powder

igniter

match heads

gasoline line

liquid oxygen line

combustion chamber

exhaust nozzle

Figure 3

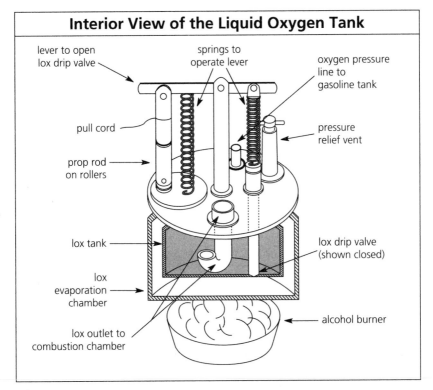

Interior View of the Liquid Oxygen Tank

lever to open
lox drip valve

springs to
operate lever

oxygen pressure
line to
gasoline tank

pull cord

pressure
relief vent

prop rod
on rollers

lox tank

lox drip valve
(shown closed)

lox
evaporation
chamber

lox outlet to
combustion chamber

alcohol burner

Figure 4

closed the pressure relief vent on the lox tank and set fire to the alcohol-soaked cotton in the burner. Immediately, Goddard began pumping oxygen from the cylinder to the propellant tanks. The pressure of the oxygen forced the gasoline and lox into the combustion chamber where the igniter was still burning. There was a loud "whoosh" as the rocket fired.

For the next 90 seconds, Goddard waited until the rocket motor's thrust exceeded its weight. It rose a few inches from the ground, held back only by the hose. Using a long rope, Goddard pulled a hinged lever that yanked the hose away and simultaneously released a spring-loaded valve. When the valve snapped shut, lox began to drip into the heated chamber surrounding the lox tank. Instantly, the lox flashed into vapor, creating the pressure necessary to force the liquids into the combustion chamber.

As soon as he pulled the lever, Goddard ran for cover behind the barricade where Percy Roope already stood. Henry Sachs was still running for cover when the rocket gave off a sharp, popping sound. A blast of white vapor and flame shot out of the nozzle. For an instant, the rocket remained motionless. Then, with a deep roar, it left its frame and climbed upward toward the blue winter sky, rising slowly at first and then picking up tremendous speed. Two-and-a-half seconds later, the roar and the jet stream suddenly ceased. Still traveling at top speed, the rocket veered to the left and

Goddard standing beside the first successful liquid-propellant rocket, shown here in the frame from which it was fired on March 16, 1926, in Auburn, Massachusetts. (Goddard Collection/Clark University)

smashed to earth in a patch of ice 184 feet away. In its short flight, the rocket had achieved an altitude of 41 feet and had reached a speed of about 60 miles per hour. Unfortunately, by the time the rocket left its frame, Esther's seven-second camera had run out of film, so there were no pictures of the actual flight.

Nevertheless, in a few brief moments, the small rocket had made history. It was the first successful flight of a liquid-fuel rocket—a milestone event as significant and important as the first manned airplane flight achieved by the Wright brothers in 1903. A granite monument commemorating the flight now stands on the site. It reads: *Site of launching of world's first liquid propellant rocket by Dr. Robert H. Goddard, Sixteen March, 1926.*

On that cold, raw winter afternoon, however, those present experienced only a sense of disappointment. Esther Goddard said later, "At the time of the flight none of the four of us there had any sense of destiny. We had no feeling that this was something remarkable. We had hoped for a straight flight and we didn't get it."

That evening, Goddard made the following terse entry in his diary. "Went to Auburn with Mr. Sachs in morning. Esther and Mr. Roope came out at 1 P.M. Tried rocket at 2:30. It rose 41 ft, and went 184 ft, in 2.5 sec, after the lower half of nozzle had burned off. Brought materials to lab. Read Mechanics, Physics of Air, and wrote up experiment in evening."

By the next day, however, Goddard seemed more aware of the significance of what he had accomplished. His growing excitement is evident in his diary entry for that day.

March 17. The first flight with a rocket using liquid propellants was made yesterday at Aunt Effie's farm in Auburn.

The day was clear and comparatively quiet. The anemometer on the Physics lab was turning leisurely when Mr. Sachs and I left in the morning, and was turning as leisurely when we returned at 5:30 P.M.

Even though the release was pulled, the rocket did not rise at first, but the flame came out, and there was a steady roar. After a number of seconds it rose, slowly until it cleared the frame, and then at express-train speed, curving over to the left, and striking the ice and snow, still going at a rapid rate.

It looked almost magical as it rose, without any appreciably greater noise and flame, as if it said, "I've been here long enough; I think I'll be

going somewhere else, if you don't mind." Esther said that it looked like
a fairy or an aesthetic dancer, as it started off. The sky was clear, for
the most part, with large shadowy white clouds, but late in the afternoon
there was a large pink cloud in the west, over which the sun shone. Some
of the surprising things were the absence of smoke, the lack of very loud
roar, and the smallness of the flame.

Several weeks later, Goddard reported to Dr. Abbot at the
Smithsonian that his recent test proved conclusively the practicality of the liquid-propelled rocket. He explained that the reason his
rocket had reached an altitude of only 41 feet was that, because of
lack of funds, he had had to build it on a small scale. He hoped
that the Smithsonian would grant him funds to develop a rocket
large enough "to reach great altitudes," pointing out that rocket
development was becoming a national issue in Germany. "Nearly
every day," he added with a note of urgency, "I am in receipt of
requests from Germany for information and details."

Although Goddard himself was convinced of the significance of
his pioneer flight, no one in Washington seemed to recognize its
importance. Even his sponsors at the Smithsonian were unim-
pressed. After nine years of supplying funds, they had hoped for
a rocket capable of "soaring" higher than 41 feet. Anxious for more
spectacular results, they urged Goddard to build a larger rocket,
one that could achieve a much higher altitude. Could he develop
such a rocket in 12 months? they asked. They did promise to
continue portioning out small amounts of money, but nothing near
the amount Goddard really needed.

The historic flight had a different effect on Esther Goddard.
Although she had always taken an active interest in her husband's
work, she admitted that "it took this flight before I could share his
excitement. Looking back, it was the most beautiful sight in the
world, seeing the rocket take off."

Now a confirmed supporter of her husband's vision, Esther did
everything she could to help. Soon after their marriage, she had
transformed the shabby old house that had once belonged to
Goddard's grandmother into a cheerful home. She painted the
dingy walls, made chintz drapes and slipcovers for the old furni-
ture, and cleaned out several decades' worth of papers, objects,
and old clothes that were stored in the attic. She had bought an

old desk and arranged a study so that Goddard could work at home. She took care of the cleaning, cooking, shopping and banking. She scrimped and saved so that every spare penny could be devoted to her husband's research.

Now, after the historic rocket flight of March 1926, Esther's involvement in her husband's work grew. She acted as his secretary and photographer and assisted him in rocket tests, even helping to put out brush fires when the tests went awry. She organized his notes and papers and kept records of his experiments. In September 1928, Nahum Goddard, then 70 years old, lay dying of cancer. Shortly before his death, he entrusted Esther with the care of his eccentric son. Deeply moved by her father-in-law's dying words, Esther experienced a new dedication and commitment.

With Esther to look after the details of daily life, Robert Goddard found more time to relax. Sometimes his evenings were spent playing the piano or painting landscapes. Occasionally the Goddards went to the movies, especially if a comedy starring Laurel and Hardy, Harold Lloyd, or Buster Keaton was on the bill. With Esther at his side, Goddard found his shyness melting; together, they attended parties and picnics with other faculty members. Whenever someone criticized Goddard for working secretly, Esther would rush to his defense, explaining that his secrecy was "proper Yankee pride" and that her husband simply didn't like to talk much.

For a while, in response to pressure from the Smithsonian, Goddard labored to solve the problems posed by a larger rocket. His new design called for a rocket 20 times larger than his earlier rocket, and a 60-foot-high tower on which to launch it. The larger size also required alterations in design, so he refined the launching and ignition systems and devised a method for cooling the walls of the combustion chamber. This method, which relied on surrounding the chamber with a "curtain" of liquid, was one of his most amazing inventions and became a basic component of all later rockets.

Transporting and setting up the larger rocket in the launching tower posed more problems. On more than one occasion, Goddard had to borrow a horse and wagon to carry the heavy equipment across the snowy fields of Aunt Effie's farm. Her neighbors, the Burgess family, became accustomed to the sight of the professor going to and from the farm. Mrs. Burgess's son-in-law reported that "whenever he did, some member of the family would say, 'There goes Moony Goodard.' They did not take him seriously."

Goddard had no time to worry about what others thought of him; he had more serious problems on his mind. He lay awake nights, planning one modification after another, but nothing seemed to go right. Test after test ended in failure. Calmly, he described each setback in his notebooks: "Welded part was too brittle" . . . "Float stuck" . . . "Worked stopping leaks in chamber" . . . "Ran flow test but pressure did not rise rapidly enough" . . . "Safety cap blew out" . . . "Entrance tube was accidentally pulled off" . . . "Pull to operate engine required too much force" . . . "Engine did not seem to generate pressure, control lines became entangled, and chamber burned through at middle" . . . "Gas tank blew up."

In September 1927, Goddard decided that the rocket on which he was working was too ambitious—and far too expensive. He began to develop a smaller rocket which was to be only four times larger than his 1926 rocket. In the months that followed, he worked on modifying and adapting his earlier designs. There were more tests, and more failures. As flaws were discovered, he found new, innovative ways of overcoming them.

Finally, Goddard's new rocket was ready for flight testing. It was 11½ feet long and weighed 35 pounds without fuel. It had guidance vanes and it would carry a payload of recording instruments, including an aneroid barometer and thermometer. The rocket was also fitted with a parachute that was meant to open when the rocket reached the zenith, or highest point, of its flight. When the parachute opened, it would trigger a camera that was rigged to photograph the readings on the weather instruments and the altimeter; it would then carry the camera and the instruments safely back to earth.

On the morning of July 17, 1929, Robert Goddard set out once again for Aunt Effie's farm. With the help of his assistants, Henry Sachs, Albert Kisk (who was Esther's brother and a machinist), Lawrence Mansur, and Percy Roope, he spent the morning setting up the rocket in its 60-foot tower and preparing it for flight. Esther, who had sewed the rocket's parachute, was on hand and ready to film the flight with her new Kodak movie camera.

At two o'clock in the afternoon, everyone took their places. Goddard described the scene this way:

> *Dr. Roope was well in the rear of the shelter with his theodolite and stopwatch, Mrs. Goddard stood just outside the right end of the shelter, holding the Sine-Kodak camera in her hands. Beside her was Mr. Kisk, who was asked to watch the cord to the cotter pin, to make certain that it was pulled off. I came next, and to my left was Mr. Sachs, who operated the pressure-generating tank, using the two cords for that purpose. At the extreme left end of the shelter, Mr. L. Mansur was stationed, and asked to watch the behavior of the rocket as closely as possible.*

When Goddard gave the signal, Sachs lit the alcohol stove. "Thirty seconds later," Goddard wrote,

> *the igniter was fired and the next three controls were operated. Mr. Sachs then gave the rocket 125 pounds pressure. As before, I waited until the rocket had risen 3 inches, as indicated by the aluminum vanes on the rocket rising up to the white marks, 3 inches long, on the vertical ⅜-inch pipe guides. I then pulled the two releasing cords in succession. The noise did not appear to change, and I kept pulling the ¼-inch rope, thinking that the rocket had not been released, until I heard someone shout "Look out!" When I looked out of the right end of the shelter, I saw the rocket just before it hit the ground.*

Goddard was delighted. It had been a good flight. In 18½ seconds, the rocket had climbed to an altitude of 90 feet—more than twice the height of the 1926 flight—leveling off in a straight-line trajectory before suddenly veering to the right and striking the ground 171 feet from the tower. As the rocket rose skyward, spitting flames and a bright white flare, it had given off a loud roar that shattered the stillness of the hot July afternoon. The noise was punctuated by the gasoline tank, which had exploded on impact. The parachute had failed to open, but the camera and barometer were still functioning. The thermometer, however, was broken. It had been subjected to heat much higher than it could register.

While Goddard and his assistants were still hunting through the wreckage for pieces of the rocket, they heard the scream of a siren. Looking up, they saw a police car, two ambulances, and a host of automobiles racing toward them through a cloud of dust.

The police, summoned by frantic calls from neighbors who reported that a plane had crashed, were the first to arrive. While the officers inspected the scene, Goddard tried to reassure them, saying that he was only conducting "one of a series of experiments in rockets." When he asked the officers if they could keep the incident quiet, one of them replied, "Do you see these two men coming? . . . They are reporters." Sure enough, the press was on hand.

The reporters examined the blackened rocks under the launch tower, they measured and photographed the tower and shelter, and they carefully examined the wreckage of the rocket. Anxious to keep his work out of the public eye, Goddard assured them that "there was no attempt to reach the moon, or anything of such a spectacular nature. The rocket is normally noisy. . . . The test was thoroughly satisfactory; nothing exploded in the air, and there was no damage except incident to the landing."

Despite Goddard's calm explanations, the headline in the *Worcester Evening Post* that evening read

TERRIFIC EXPLOSION AS PROF. GODDARD OF CLARK SHOOTS HIS "MOON ROCKET"
WOMAN THOUGHT ROCKET WAS WRECKED AIRPLANE
Ambulance Rushed to Auburn to Care for "Victims of Crash," Find Clark Professor and Assistants Making Experiments with Rocket— Plane from Local Airport Also Made Search from Air for Reported "Victims"

The next day, the *Boston Globe* carried this headline:

"MOON ROCKET" MAN'S TEST ALARMS WHOLE COUNTRYSIDE. BLAST AS METAL PROJECTILE IS FIRED THROUGH AUBURN TOWER ECHOES FOR MILES AROUND, STARTS HUNT FOR FALLEN PLANE, AND FINALLY REVEALS GODDARD EXPERIMENT STATION

Once again, Robert Goddard, the crazy "moon man," was news. A steady stream of newspaper reporters, sightseers, and souvenir hunters besieged the launch site on Aunt Effie's farm. And if that were not bad enough, the Massachusetts fire marshal had been alerted. Afraid that Goddard's rockets might set fire to their houses and barns, the townspeople of Auburn wanted the moon rocket tests outlawed. The fire marshal agreed. Fire Marshal Neal notified

Goddard that he could no longer conduct his menacing tests in the Commonwealth of Massachusetts.

If Robert Goddard wanted to continue his experiments, he would have to find a new and very secret place in which to do so.

CHAPTER 6 NOTES

p. 60   "It looked almost magical . . ." PRHG, Vol. II, p. 581.

p. 60   "It is the same old story . . ." PRHG, Vol. II, p. 567.

p. 67   "At the time of the flight . . ." Shelly M. Lauzon, *Robert Hutchings Goddard Memorial Dedication*, p. 10.

p. 67   "Went to Auburn . . ." PRHG, Vol. II, p. 580.

pp. 67–68 "March 17. The first flight . . ." PRHG, Vol. II, p. 581.

p. 68   "Nearly every day, . . ." PRHG, Vol. II, p. 590.

p. 68   "it took this flight . . ." Milton Lehman, *This High Man*, p. 144.

p. 70   "whenever he did, . . ." Letter to the author from Robert W. Lord of New York City, son-in-law of Gertrude Giddings Burgess, a neighbor of Effie Ward.

p. 70   "Welded part was brittle . . ." PRHG, Vol. II, pp. 601–15.

p. 71   "Dr. Roope was well . . ." PRHG, Vol. II, p. 668.

p. 72   "one of a series . . ." PRHG, Vol. II, p. 671.

p. 72   "there was no attempt . . ." PRHG, Vol. II, pp. 671–72.

p. 72   "TERRIFIC EXPLOSION . . ." PRHG, Vol. II, p. 92.

p. 72   "'MOON ROCKET' MAN'S TEST . . ." PRHG, Vol. II, p. 93.

7

LUCKY LINDY

"We live in a world where dreams and reality interchange."
—Charles A. Lindbergh

Robert Goddard felt trapped. Where could he find the quiet, out-of-the-way place he needed to continue his experiments? His rocket tests had been banned in Massachusetts, but he couldn't afford to move. If he left Massachusetts, he would have to give up his job at Clark University. Then he remembered Camp Devens, a War Department training camp situated about 25 miles from Auburn. It was owned by the federal government and was, therefore, outside the jurisdiction of the Massachusetts fire marshal.

Goddard appealed to Dr. Abbot at the Smithsonian for help. "It will hardly be possible to continue the work unless the tests can be carried out in a location from which trespassers can be barred, and where there is no chance of danger to private property," he wrote. "With this situation in mind, I took a trip recently to Camp Devens . . . [and] located a place which looks promising. . . . If you could arrange with the authorities in Washington so that we could have the use of this spot and have Government no-trespassing signs posted . . . I think it would be as near an ideal arrangement as we could have for the next tests."

After Dr. Abbot explained Goddard's predicament to the War Department, permission was granted on the condition that all tests were to be conducted only after the ground was rain-soaked or covered with snow, and that fire extinguishers were kept on hand. So, in October 1929, Goddard moved his test site to an artillery range at Camp Devens. He dismantled the launch tower at Aunt

Effie's and set it up near a stagnant pool, appropriately named Hell Pond, at the far end of the range. It was a long drive from the laboratory at Clark, and the roads leading to the new launch site were filled with bone-jarring ruts that often put his apparatus out of order. Whenever that happened, he had to spend hours making repairs. The arrangement was far from "ideal," but if Goddard was discouraged, he never showed it.

Late one dismal Friday afternoon in November 1929, Goddard was sitting at his desk in his office at Clark when the telephone rang. He could hardly believe it when the caller announced his name: Charles A. Lindbergh. Two years before, Lindbergh had thrilled the world by flying over the Atlantic Ocean from New York to Paris. It was the first nonstop flight linking the two continents, and he had flown it alone in his small airplane, *The Spirit of St. Louis.* His daring feat had earned him the admiration of the nation and inspired a generation of young dreamers. He was called America's greatest flight pioneer, and his adoring fans nicknamed him Lucky Lindy.

Despite his fame, Lindbergh was a modest, shy young man, and he addressed Goddard with admiration and respect. He told the older man that he had read the sensational newspaper accounts of Goddard's latest rocket test and of his problems with the Massachusetts fire marshal, and he was interested in learning more. He had given much thought to the limitations of propeller-driven aircraft and believed that rockets and jet propulsion might someday be used on airplanes. Would it be all right, he asked, if he drove to Worcester the following morning for a visit? Goddard was stunned, but he quickly agreed.

It took only a few moments for Lindbergh and Goddard to realize that they liked each other immensely. Although Goddard was 20 years older than his famous visitor, they soon discovered that they were much alike. Both were "lone eagles," men of integrity and honor, who shared a vision of humanity's future in space.

Goddard found himself talking freely about his work to the shy young flier. He had never before met someone who understood so well what he was trying to accomplish. He talked easily about his recent experiments and, with a small measure of pride, screened the films of his test flights. He told Lindbergh that he was developing plans for a rocket that could reach altitudes of 100 miles and more above the Earth, and he explained how a multistage rocket could someday reach the moon. He spoke of his most secret dream—the dream of traveling far above the Earth to the distant stars beyond.

Years later, Lindbergh recalled that first meeting.

> Sitting in his home in Worcester, Massachusetts, in 1929, I listened to Robert Goddard outline his ideas for the future development of rockets—what might be practically expected, what might be eventually achieved. Thirty years later, watching a giant rocket rise above the Air Force test base at Cape Canaveral, I wondered whether he was dreaming then or I was dreaming now.

As Goddard spoke, the line dividing science from science fiction seemed to melt away. It was clear that Goddard had worked out his theories carefully on paper, and Lindbergh was convinced that it was only a matter of time—and money—before the older man's dream was transformed into reality. He wanted to assist in any way he could.

When Lindbergh asked what would help Goddard most in carrying out his experiments, the professor answered that, more than anything else, he wanted to be free of the classroom duties that took up so much of his time. Next, he wanted a place where he could test his rockets without interference and without bothering anyone.

Then Lindbergh asked how much money he might need. After a few moments, Goddard replied that if he could obtain a grant of $25,000 a year for four years, he would be able to cover the costs of all expenses, including salaries for himself and one or two assistants, as well as materials, equipment, transportation, and so on. "Under such circumstances," Lindbergh later wrote, "he felt he could accomplish within forty-eight months what might otherwise take a lifetime. He spoke as though such an amount was part of a dream beyond realization."

There was no question that Goddard needed money, and that he needed it soon. His latest Smithsonian grant was nearly exhausted, and there seemed little prospect of getting more funds from that source. If he could not find a new source of financial support quickly, his work would grind to a halt.

Lindbergh, realizing the obstacles that Goddard faced, hinted that it might be possible to get the help he needed. After

Lindbergh's departure, Goddard remembered the young man's words with hope. Although he had not expressed his fears to Lindbergh, he was deeply worried about what might happen when his meager funds were depleted. He would have to close down his laboratory. His assistants would have to find work elsewhere. And what would he do if he could not work on his rockets? The prospect of abandoning his work was too terrible to contemplate.

But Lindbergh seemed to sense the urgency. He wasted no time in seeking support for his new friend. A few days later, he called Goddard again, saying that he had set up an appointment for the next day with Henry du Pont at the Du Pont Corporation in Wilmington, Maryland. Within a few hours, Goddard found himself on a train to Wilmington.

"Colonel Lindbergh said he believed the Du Pont Company would perhaps be willing to contribute very substantial support if the applications to aircraft could be made clear," Goddard reported in a letter to Dr. Abbot. But when the Du Pont engineers questioned him about the construction of his rockets, Goddard grew suspicious. "I realized soon that the object of this questioning was not so much to determine what could be done on airplanes as to find every last detail of the rocket I have developed during the last nine years, and after I saw this I evaded further questions."

Although nothing resulted from the conference with Henry du Pont and his engineering staff, the trip to Wilmington was memorable. After the meeting, Lindbergh offered to fly Goddard to New York, from which point he could continue on to Massachusetts by train. It was Goddard's first trip in an airplane, and Lindbergh later recalled that the older man had seemed "strangely distracted" during the flight. Lindbergh's plane was a small two-seater, and as he demonstrated the craft's capabilities to his passenger, Goddard seemed to grow even more quiet. The professor, who dreamed of soaring to the moon, was happy to be flying with the world's most famous aviator, but he wasn't prepared for all those thrilling loops and dives. "He [took] me up to 8000 feet, and down to within 50 feet of the tops of the pine trees, the latter proving a good test of my nerve," Goddard later recalled.

Lindbergh's next step was to arrange a conference with Dr. John C. Merriam, president of the Carnegie Institution in Washington, on December 10, 1929. Also present were Dr. Abbot of the Smithsonian, Dr. W. S. Adams and Dr. Harold D. Babcock of the Mount Wilson Observatory, and Dr. C. F. Martin, who was chief of the U.S. Weather Bureau. Lindbergh opened the meeting with an inspiring introduction in which he said that he believed that the limit of speed had very nearly been reached with present airplanes, "making a new method [the rocket] necessary, but also saying that the proper way to advance the work would be to develop the scientific uses first, in a study of the atmosphere." Lindbergh agreed with Goddard that any talk of other objectives, such as sending rockets to the moon, would frighten off prospective donors.

Then Goddard spoke about his work, outlining the principles of the high-altitude rocket, and describing his recent experiments with liquid fuels. Dr. Abbot followed with a speech in which he gave high praise to Goddard's accomplishments and stressed their value to both aeronautics and national defense.

The men gathered at the meeting were excited. Questions followed: How high could Goddard's rocket go? How much would it cost? Goddard hesitated for a moment before replying that "judging from the expense and time so far, $100,000 would not be too much to speed the work along."

At the conclusion of the meeting, it was apparent to everyone that Goddard was no "crackpot" but was, instead, a serious and gifted scientist whose work deserved substantial support. Unfortunately, the Carnegie Institution's budget was not large. The directors, however, did agree to give him a $5,000 grant.

Goddard accepted the grant gratefully, but Lindbergh was disappointed. He thought that their next step should be to approach a financier, one with enough vision and courage to risk money on a wild rocket scheme. Times were hard—a few months before, the stock market had crashed, ushering in an era of prolonged economic depression—but Lindbergh was sure he could find someone to provide Goddard with research funds.

Although the Carnegie grant was welcome, Goddard felt that the meeting had produced a more important, if less tangible, result. Suddenly, it seemed, scientists all over the country began to pay attention to his work. Professors who had spoken skeptically of

Goddard's rockets now invited him to address their classes. But although the recognition of his fellow scientists was gratifying, it would not pay his bills.

When the last of the grant from the Smithsonian was used up, Goddard felt that an important period in his life had come to a close. He wrote a long letter of appreciation to his old sponsor, Dr. Abbot, thanking the Smithsonian for the support it had given to his rocket work "from its start as a bare idea with little experimental verification." In a more personal tone, he added, "I am also particularly grateful for your interest, encouragement, and far-sightedness . . . when hardly anyone else in the world could see anything of importance in the undertaking."

Fortunately, he had the Carnegie grant, which, although small, allowed Goddard to continue his work at Camp Devens. His spare time after classes that winter was spent improving the performance of his rocket engine while reducing its weight. "In my tests," he wrote in a letter to John C. Merriam, "the ratio has been about 200 horsepower per pound, as compared with 1 horsepower per pound, for the best airplane engine. Not only this, but with the weight reduction that appears possible, this ratio should be as high as 500 horsepower per pound of engine." He had also increased the gas ejection velocity from 4,000 to 6,000 pounds.

But despite his success, Goddard continued to worry. It was May 1930. He had not heard from Colonel Lindbergh in months, and he still did not have the money he needed. He was ready to begin testing on a larger scale, but it would be difficult to conduct tests at Hell Pond. During the summer months, Camp Devens was used as a military training ground. He was also afraid that his assistants would leave. After all, they needed to be paid if they were to stay with him.

But Lindbergh had not forgotten about his friend. He was, in fact, determined to find support for Goddard—and find it he did. On May 29, 1930, he called the professor with wonderful news. He had approached the wealthy Guggenheim family on Goddard's behalf. They had agreed to set aside $100,000 to fund Goddard over the next four years. He would send a letter to Goddard confirming all the details.

Goddard could hardly believe it. He rushed into the kitchen where Esther was preparing dinner. Now they might be able to get

Charles A. Lindbergh, an ardent supporter of Goddard's research, standing near the professor's launching tower in September 1935. (Goddard Collection/Clark University)

the equipment and time they needed, he told her. Now they would be able to move wherever they wanted. The news called for a celebration. Esther quickly put the food away; it would keep for another day. That evening, the Goddards cautiously celebrated their future over egg rolls and chow mein at Hong Fong's Chinese Restaurant.

Lucky Lindy had flown into Robert Goddard's life and brought him the luck he so desperately needed.

CHAPTER 7 NOTES

p. 74   "We live in a world . . ." Milton Lehman, *This High Man*, p. xiii.

p. 74   "It will hardly be possible . . ." PRHG, Vol. II, pp. 683–84.

p. 76   "Sitting in his home . . ." Milton Lehman, *This High Man*, p. xiii.

p. 76   "Under such circumstances . . ." Milton Lehman, *This High Man*, p. 162.

p. 77   "Colonel Lindbergh said he believed . . ." PRHG, Vol. II, pp. 714–715.

p. 77   "He [took] me up . . ." PRHG, Vol. I, p. 32.

p. 78   "making a new method . . ." PRHG, Vol. II, p. 723.

p. 78   "judging from the expense . . ." PRHG, Vol. II, p. 725.

p. 79   "from its start . . ." PRHG, Vol. II, p. 742.

p. 79   "In my tests, . . ." PRHG, Vol. II, p. 741.

8

THE DESERT

"How many years I shall be able to work on the problem, I do not know; I hope, as long as I live. There can be no thought of finishing, for 'aiming at the stars,' both literally and figuratively, is a problem to occupy generations, so that no matter how much progress one makes, there is always the thrill of just beginning."
—Dr. Robert H. Goddard

Shortly before his famous transatlantic flight, Charles Lindbergh had met Harry Guggenheim, a former World War I naval pilot and a member of one of America's wealthiest families. Harry had convinced his father, Daniel Guggenheim, that airplanes were the wave of the future, and the old man, excited by the possibilities that lay ahead in air travel, had set up the Daniel Guggenheim Fund for the Promotion of Aeronautics. The fund, which was administered by Harry Guggenheim, offered grants to universities engaged in aeronautics research and was instrumental in making flight popular, promoting passenger aircraft, and improving safety. Because of their shared interests, it seemed only natural that the two young men became close friends.

At first, Lindbergh was reluctant to impose on his friendship with the Guggenheims, but the more he thought about Robert Goddard's plight, the more his reluctance melted. He called on Daniel Guggenheim and urged him to support the reclusive rocket scientist. "This professor of yours, he seems capable?" Guggenheim asked. Lindbergh assured him that Goddard knew more about rockets than anybody else in the country. "Do you think it's worth my investing $100,000?" Guggenheim asked bluntly. Yes, answered Lindbergh, yes, it's worth it.

Guggenheim, impressed by Lindbergh's faith in the professor, agreed to accept Goddard's estimate of his expenses and to put no restrictions on his activities. Guggenheim's only requirement was that Goddard periodically report on his progress to a committee that would include Dr. Abbot of the Smithsonian, Charles Lindbergh, and several scientists. He set aside $50,000, to be given to Goddard in equal installments of $25,000 for the next two years. If, at the end of two years, the committee was sufficiently impressed by the professor's progress, another $50,000 would be made available. The money would be channeled through Clark University as a special "Daniel Guggenheim Fund for the Measurement and Investigation of High Altitudes." Compared with the costs of rocket development in later years, it was a small sum, but at the time, it was a huge amount to give to a single, private scientist. It was certainly more money than Goddard had ever dared to hope for. It was a dream come true.

In a mood of elation, Goddard lost no time in requesting a leave of absence from Clark University. Although President Atwood of Clark was sorry to see Goddard leave, he wished the professor well and offered to lend him most of the equipment in the university's physics shop.

Goddard immediately gathered his crew together and told them the good news. Would they join him in the new enterprise? The project, he estimated, would take about two years, and he didn't yet know where they would be going. Without hesitation, Henry Sachs, Albert Kisk, Larry Mansur, and Charles Mansur agreed to follow Goddard wherever he went.

With the help of his crew, Goddard quickly dismantled the launch tower at Camp Devens. By June 24, 1930, everything was ready. That evening, he wrote in his diary that he had "looked over Longfellow's *Daybreak* in the afternoon." The poem begins,

A wind came up out of the sea,
And said, "O mists, make room for me!"
It hailed the ships, and cried, "Sail on,
Ye mariners, the night is gone!"
And hurried landward far away,
Crying, "Awake! it is the day!"

He was tired but exhilarated. His launch tower, rocket parts, machine tools, and equipment were packed into wooden crates ready for shipment. He did not know where he was going, or what the future might hold, but it seemed to Robert Goddard that his day had finally dawned.

His first step was to find a suitable location for rocket launchings. With the help of Colonel Lindbergh and Dr. Charles F. Brooks, a meteorologist at Clark, Goddard studied weather and climate maps. He was looking for a high region with a minimum of rain and snowfall, clear skies, and no fog—a place with few extremes in temperature and with long periods of windless days. He also needed good, level ground, and lots of it. Above all, he wanted a place where few people lived, so that his rockets could roar, crash, and even explode without endangering or alarming anyone.

The high plateau located in the southeast corner of New Mexico seemed to fulfill all his requirements. It was desert country, with long, sunny days and clear, star-filled nights. The climate was warm enough to permit flights all year round. When Dr. Brooks told him that the Weather Bureau had a station in the town of Roswell and that there were people there who might be of help to him, Goddard narrowed his search.

A few days later, on July 15, 1930, Robert and Esther Goddard set off for New Mexico in a newly purchased secondhand red Packard coupé. "I shall decide on a location after I arrive," he wrote to Lindbergh, "and then have the men, machinery, and supplies follow."

In the days before the interstate highway system was built, crossing the United States by automobile was a long and sometimes hazardous journey. The 2,500-mile trip was an adventure for the Goddards, especially for Esther, who had never before ventured out of New England. In letters to her family, she described the changing landscape as each mile took them further from the neat, comfortable towns of the Northeast through the vast midwestern farmlands to the bleak, haunting desert that lay at journey's end.

As soon as he explored the town and checked weather conditions with the local meteorologist, Goddard knew that Roswell, New Mexico, was the ideal base for his operations. Set on a high plateau 3,600 feet above sea level, the town lay just west of the Pecos River and served as a center for sheep and cattle ranchers. It had paved, tree-shaded streets, with plenty of well-stocked stores, banks, and a movie house to serve its population of 11,000. The Santa Fe Railroad made daily stops, so it would not be difficult to get needed supplies.

Because of its ideal climate, Roswell also housed a colony of tuberculosis patients. Esther, increasingly concerned about Goddard's health, hoped that the clear, pure air would help her husband as well. He had recently been denied life insurance after a doctor listened to his rattled breathing and pronounced that "he ought to be in bed in Switzerland." (At that time, TB was treated mainly with clean country air, as might be found in the Swiss countryside.) Tuberculosis bacilli still lurked in Goddard's lungs.

Aside from being an ideal place for rocket experiments, Roswell, with old pioneer trails running through it, had a colorful Wild West history that also appealed to Goddard. Gunslingers like Billy the Kid had made their reputations here, and wagon trains had once passed through on their lonesome westward journeys. Goddard sensed a spirit that matched his own. He was a pioneer too—a pioneer of a new order, the first of many who would come to the New Mexico desert to conquer distant worlds. Ten years later, atomic scientists would begin their tests at Los Alamos, and still later, the army would set up rocket proving grounds at White Sands.

By early August, Goddard had rented a large, furnished ranch house three miles outside the town. Although the Mescalero Ranch needed repairs, it was ideally situated in an isolated spot at the end of a road. Goddard quickly notified his crew in Massachusetts; they arrived by train a few days later, along with a boxcar filled with equipment. There was no need for them to find housing; the ranch house was large enough to accommodate everyone. As soon as they unpacked, the crew set to work building a machine shop, while the professor went scouting for a place on which to erect the launch tower.

Goddard found it on some open range land about 10 miles from the ranch. He approached the owner, a rancher named Oscar White, and cautiously explained that he needed a place to shoot off rockets. White apparently liked Goddard; he told the professor that he could use "that nice little field"—a level 16,000-acre stretch of barren land called Eden Valley—rent free. By October 19, Anniversary Day, the tower was up, anchored in place by guy wires and concrete.

The machine shop was ready, too. It contained lathes, milling machines, drills, grinders, welders, and a variety of other tools, as well as Goddard's old desk and a workbench where he sometimes made small models out of scrap metal to demonstrate his ideas to his assistants.

About 100 feet from the machine shop, Goddard and his assistants had erected a small static test frame so that rocket models could undergo repeated static tests before they were launched into flight. When the fuel was ignited, the rocket was held in the frame by heavy, water-filled oil drums connected to an apparatus that measured the rocket's thrust. The scorching blasts from the rockets were directed downward into a concrete trough, called "the bathtub," constructed under the frame. When the rockets were ready for flight, Goddard and his assistants hauled them out to the launching site in Eden Valley.

The shop was crude, and so were living conditions at the Mescalero Ranch. The house, which had been vacant for several years, needed fixing, and a new well had to be dug. Everyone pitched in, cleaning, repairing, doing what had to be done. Esther, as she was to do throughout their stay in the desert, took care of the house and cooked all the meals while continuing to act as her husband's assistant. Outdoors, in the harsh, barren desert, rattlesnakes, scorpions, and other strange creatures posed a threat. But everyone was happy to be there, especially Goddard.

Freed at last from his teaching duties and from money worries, Goddard was able, for the first time in his life, to devote all his time to his rocket projects. He lost no time in outlining his priorities. First, he wanted to build a more powerful, lightweight, rocket motor capable of withstanding the high temperatures generated in the combustion chamber. Then, he would work on the steering and gyroscopic stabilization systems so that the rocket could maintain vertical flight without veering off course. He would also develop a parachute mechanism so that the rocket could be recovered and its parts reused. Finally, he would design new pressure pumps to feed the combustion chamber.

Goddard was eager to launch at least one rocket before the end of the year. On October 29, 1930, he conducted his first static test at Roswell. The nozzle stuck, and the gas tank exploded. More tests followed, each revealing a new flaw.

His mechanics grew impatient, but Goddard never seemed perturbed. When he explained with gentle humor how each failure contained a lesson and calmly went about redesigning a valve or a nozzle, their morale was restored. They found "the professor" to be a kind, gentle man, easy to work with and completely approachable—but their feelings for him went beyond admiration and respect. Although he never complained about his health, they knew he was frail, and they felt warm and protective toward him. Still, it was hard to get close to Goddard, he was so private and restrained, and it was even more difficult to understand the source of his iron determination, his strength of purpose. It seemed to them that Goddard was blessed with a vision and a genius beyond that of other men, and they willingly let him lead them.

By Thanksgiving, Goddard was working on a new pressure-feeding plan. If all went well, Little Nell (as they had fondly nicknamed the rocket) would soon be ready. Esther made dinner, and with the whole group assembled around the dining table, Goddard proposed a toast: "Here's to our little Nell, may she grow more and more flighty."

Finally, on December 30, Little Nell was ready for testing. It was a small model of the rocket he had planned for 20 years. It measured 11 feet long and weighed 33.5 pounds. Early in the morning, Goddard and his crew packed it carefully onto a trailer attached to a Model T Ford, covered it with old quilts, and set out for the Eden Valley launch site. Esther, with her motion picture camera, followed a few hours later. By mid-afternoon, the rocket was in place on the launching frame. The crew was tense, but Goddard's face showed no emotion. Privately, however, he prayed that the rocket would perform as planned. His highest flight so far had been less than one hundred feet. If the combustion chamber on this rocket held, it might achieve a much higher altitude.

When Goddard gave the word, the launch sequence began. As the pressure tanks built up to 225 pounds, the rocket seemed to strain against the cables. It was time to pull the release levers. The rocket rose, slowly at first but gradually increasing in speed. As it cleared the top of the tower, it suddenly shot up into the high desert sky. Straight as an arrow, the rocket rose, the sun glinting off its polished nose cone. Moving at 500 miles an hour, it did not stop climbing until it reached 2,000 feet—the highest altitude attained so far by any of Goddard's rockets. He watched for the parachute to open, but something must have jammed. Seven seconds after countdown, the rocket fell with a shrill whistle, plunging to earth 1,000 feet away.

The crew was thrilled, but Goddard wasted no time in self-congratulation. He decided that as soon as they had gathered up the wreckage, he would attack the problem of the parachute release and work on the gyroscopic controls. That night, he briefly noted the results of the flight in his diary, adding, "went to Princess Theatre with E., in evening, and saw *Billy the Kid.*"

Unfortunately, Goddard could not share the good news with his sponsor. He had hoped to present the old man with concrete results, but Daniel Guggenheim had passed away before Goddard outlined his progress to the committee in a February 1931 meeting in Washington, D.C. The Guggenheim committee, however, was highly impressed with his progress. The flight, Goddard explained, proved that a light, very high speed rocket could be made for obtaining records, and for other uses, at a few thousand feet. But the attainment of greater heights, he added, could not be accomplished without the use of automatic stabilization. He planned, he said, to proceed at once with more research into automatically stabilized flight. "Just . . . when we can expect a really high flight, I cannot say. I feel certain, however, that it will be a number of months," he concluded optimistically.

Privately, however, Goddard was troubled by malfunctions in the combustion chamber's "curtain cooling" system. Sometimes it worked, but when it didn't the motor burned up. He tried spraying the inner side of the chamber wall with various ratios of lox and gasoline, he modified the holes through which the liquids were fed, and he varied the angles at which the liquids were injected. As often as not, the system failed to work and the intense heat burned through the thin chamber walls. Until new ceramics and alloys were invented, the problem remained a challenge to later rocket experimenters.

While he struggled with the cooling system, Goddard also conducted experiments to achieve higher velocities. He found that the key factor was the relationship between the size of the combustion chamber and the amount of fuel it burned. He would have to approach the problem gradually, increasing the size of his rockets step by step, and making sure each one worked before constructing a larger rocket.

As the rockets grew larger, so did the need to improve the system for maintaining pressure in the lox and gasoline tanks. The ideal solution would be a small, powerful pump—but no such pump existed, nor did he have time to develop one. Goddard decided, instead, to use a tank of compressed nitrogen, fitted with a pressure regulator, so that the pressure of the gas would force the liquids into the chamber. He spent weeks building a regulator that would allow just enough pressure to force the liquids, but not enough to blow up the rocket.

In whatever spare time he had, Goddard worked on the design of a gyroscopic stabilizer. "It was decided to attack this problem of stabilization," he wrote, "by developing a system of movable steering vanes that could be pushed, by the controlling action of a gyroscope, into the blast of hot gases that rushes out of the end of the rocket. Acting on the vane, the powerful blast would shove the rocket's nose back toward the vertical. It had to be a complicated device—a veritable mechanical brain directing mechanical muscles . . . but as with all other rocket features, weight was a vital factor."

The special characteristic of a gyroscope is that it resists any change in position once it has been set into motion. By harnessing this ability, Goddard was able to develop an efficient steering mechanism for his rocket. The gyroscope was positioned so that its axis was parallel to the axis of the rocket as it stood upright in the launch tower. Just before launching, the gyroscope was set in motion. When the rocket took off, the gyroscope prevented it from veering off its vertical course. If the rocket tilted, the gyroscope triggered a piston that forced the vanes into the slipstream jetting out of the end of the rocket, thereby

Goddard (second from right) and his assistants holding the first gyroscopically controlled rocket, used in the flight of April 19, 1932. The guiding vanes were made comparatively small to avoid overcorrecting the flight. (Goddard Collection/Clark University)

causing the rocket to correct its course. The gyroscopic stabilizer, which he later patented, was one of Goddard's most ingenious inventions and is used on all large rockets today.

On April 19, 1932, after a long series of tests, Goddard launched his first gyroscopically controlled rocket. After a brief flight, the rocket turned earthward and crashed. Goddard was disappointed but not discouraged. Rushing to the wreckage, he found the four vanes. The one that should have been forced into the slipstream was warm. The other three were cold. It proved that the gyroscope had worked properly.

The following day, Goddard revealed his feelings in a letter to H. G. Wells, whose book *The War of the Worlds* he had first read when he was 16 and had reread once a year ever since. "What I find most inspiring is your optimism," he wrote. "It is the best antidote I know for the feeling of depression that comes at times when one contemplates the remarkable capacity for bungling of both man and nature."

A few weeks later, Goddard launched another rocket, this time with disastrous results. The combustion chamber burned up, both the parachute and the gyroscope failed to work, and the rocket ended up a smoking ruin. Something had gone wrong in Eden Valley, and Goddard made plans to correct it. But another flight would not take place. Something had gone wrong in the nation, too—something that would put a halt to his work. It was the last test Goddard would make in Roswell for a long time to come.

CHAPTER 8 NOTES

p. 82   "How many years . . ." PRHG, Vol. II, p. 823.

p. 82   "This professor of yours, . . ." Milton Lehman, *This High Man*, p. 174.

p. 83   "looked over Longfellow's *Daybreak* . . ." PRHG, Vol. II, p. 747.

p. 87   "Here's to our Little Nell, . . ." PRHG, Vol. II, p. 778.

p. 88   "went to Princess Theatre . . ." PRHG, Vol. II, p. 778.

p. 88   "Just . . . when we can expect . . ." Milton Lehman, *This High Man*, p. 191.

p. 89   "It was decided to attack . . ." PRHG, Vol. II, p. 810.

p. 90   "What I find most inspiring . . ." PRHG, Vol. II, p. 823.

9

COUNTDOWN TO SUCCESS

"Emerson says, 'If a man paint a better picture, preach a better sermon, or build a better mousetrap than anyone else, the world will make a beaten path to his door.' I, like many others, have had the misfortune not to be an artist, a preacher, or a manufacturer of mousetraps."

—Dr. Robert H. Goddard

It hadn't taken Robert Goddard very long to settle into a new life in New Mexico. Although the landscape was vastly different from that of his native New England, he felt happy and at home. There was something about the high, lonely desert, with its limitless expanse of sky, that matched his own restless, yearning spirit. At night, the brilliant stars seemed close enough to touch. Come, they seemed to beckon, come! With an artist's eye, he observed the subtlest changes in the land around him. "Dark blue clouds in afternoon, break in them was lemon yellow, with redder patches . . . distant blue thunderheads, with yellow edges, could be seen through the clouds." In his spare moments, he set up an easel to capture the magic in oils on canvas.

Once installed, Goddard felt no need to leave the Mescalero Ranch. His days were spent coming and going between the house, the shop, and the test site, and that was all he needed. He packed away the conservative blue suits and starched collars that had been his "professor's uniform" and dressed instead in comfortable slacks and open-necked shirts that were more suitable for working in the desert heat. When it was time to pick up the mail, or when

Mescalero Ranch, 1936. In rare moments of relaxation, Goddard painted desert landscapes. A local artist said of Goddard that "he approached the outrageous contrasts of New Mexican color with considerable gusto," but "what mattered most to him was not what he drew, but what happened inside him—that deep, almost religious feeling that touches every artist." (Goddard Collection/Clark University)

supplies were needed for the house or the shop, it was Esther who drove into town alone.

People in Roswell were curious about the secretive professor and what he might be "up to," but Goddard resisted any invasion of his privacy. When reporters showed up at the ranch, he politely declined to give interviews. And when the Roswell Rotary Club asked him to speak, he accepted the invitation but gave a speech that revealed nothing about his work.

The only interruptions came from the chest colds that seemed to be attacking him with increasing frequency. Annoyed when the local doctor confined him to bed, he nevertheless used these periods of enforced rest to work on designs for new components. Later, he would discover that these "colds" signaled a return of his old enemy, tuberculosis.

But nothing, not even ill health, could stop Goddard. By the spring of 1932, he had made spectacular progress. He hoped that when he outlined his results to the Guggenheim committee, they would in turn authorize the additional $50,000 they had promised for two more years of research.

But 1932 was an unlucky year. The Great Depression had worsened, and all across the country, people were suffering. Banks failed, factories shut their doors, and people lost their homes. At the same time, drought was turning fertile farms into a dust bowl. Breadlines tried to feed the hungry and homeless, while 13 million unemployed roamed the country seeking work.

Isolated as they were, the Goddards were barely touched by events that affected other Americans. But they did not remain so for long. In March came the shocking news that Charles Lindbergh's son had been kidnapped. The nation prayed for the safety of their hero's child, but two months later, the little boy's murdered body was found. Lucky Lindy's good fortune had deserted him. Goddard's luck was about to vanish as well.

In May 1932, Goddard traveled to Washington, D.C., to report on his progress to the Guggenheim committee. They were very impressed with what he had accomplished and assured him that they thought his work should continue. But then they shook their heads and, with reluctance and some embarrassment, denied his request for additional funds. Henry Breckinridge, the Guggenheim attorney, explained the state of affairs. The stock market crash had eroded the Guggenheim estate, he said. Maybe in a year or two funds would be available, but for right now, there was no money.

Just as he did whenever a rocket test failed, Robert Goddard took this setback in stride. "I think you are a good sport to take such a disappointment with so much courage and philosophy," Breckinridge wrote to him. Many years later, Breckinridge remembered Goddard this way: "You couldn't possibly stop him. He was indomitable. He had restraint, self-respect and a faith that would move mountains. He behaved as if he had all the time he needed to carry out his work."

As always, Goddard did what had to be done. The hardest task was telling his crew the bad news: with no money, they would have to close up shop. The tools, machinery, and old parts were packed into crates. Some were shipped off to Clark University and the rest were stored in the warehouse of a local hardware store. Next, Goddard and his crew gathered up all the discarded pieces of old rockets, hammered them beyond recognition, and buried them deep in the desert sand. When the work of dismantling was over, Goddard gave each man a letter of recommendation and said he would call on them whenever his grant was renewed. Finally, when the house and shop were boarded up, it was time to leave. Esther and Robert Goddard piled into their coupé and headed eastward. Behind them, hidden away in the vast expanse of Eden Valley, the abandoned launch tower stood like a lonely sentinel frozen in time.

By the end of July, 1932, the Goddards were back in their old house on Maple Hill. In September, Goddard resumed teaching at Clark. On October 5, he let his 50th birthday pass without a mention in his diary, but on October 19 he wrote, "Went to the cherry tree." Once again, he seemed to draw strength from a visit to the site of his original inspiration.

He was back to his old routine of teaching, doing his own work in his spare time—without his crew and without a testing ground. His experiments had been halted as he stood on the verge of a breakthrough. No one would have been surprised if he had given way to despair. But that was not the case. Goddard went on as though nothing had happened. If he could not flight-test his rockets, he would spend his time refining the gyroscopic stabilization system and generally finding ways to reduce the weight of the entire rocket—things that would have to be done if his rockets were ever to reach very high altitudes. Dr. Abbot of the Smithsonian managed to scrape up a grant of $250 to pay for supplies. It wasn't much, but it would help to keep the work going.

No one, not even Esther, could detect any outward change in the professor. Only in his private diary did Goddard hint at the doubts that sometimes threatened him. "All fame is relative," he wrote. "Happiness comes from struggling and overcoming difficulties . . . If you handle the present sensibly and properly, the future will take care of itself . . . Never worry about what you cannot change . . . Yesterday is gone; you have today; tomorrow may never come."

Instead of feeling sorry for himself, Goddard immersed himself in work and, over the course of the next two years, he produced a prodigious amount in his spare time. He invented a better method of gyroscopic steering, an ingenious centrifugal pump, pumps for rocket propellants, igniters, fuel injection devices, and heat insulators. He developed new ways to weld and bolt joints, and explored lightweight alloys. He filled his notebooks with ideas for solar and ion motors, nose cones, pressure gauges, resonating chambers, and scores of other devices. "Perfectly amazing how things come to you," he wrote in his diary. "All you have to do is think about things long enough and, pop! something bursts and there it is."

By the end of 1934, he had secured patents on 26 inventions, including two—"Apparatus for Igniting Liquid Fuel," which described his "curtain cooling" method, and "Mechanism for Directing Flight," which outlined his method of gyroscopic steering—that were later incorporated into the design of the German V-2 rocket. Although German rocket scientists later maintained that they had developed these components independently, the charge that they copied Goddard's design is well founded. Soon after these two patents were issued in September 1932, the patent office was besieged with requests for copies from abroad. Later examinations of the V-2 rocket revealed only minor alterations in the designs of the components covered by Goddard's patents.

Goddard himself was growing more and more suspicious of the persistent letters from German scientists that crowded his mailbox. He answered all with unfailing courtesy, but he refused to disclose any information about his work.

Although he had no way of knowing why, Goddard had good cause to be wary. In 1934, Adolf Hitler rose to power as Führer, and the German war machine was set in motion. Rocket scientists Wernher von Braun and Walter Dornberger, with a staff of 80 fellow scientists, were already at work. A few years later, at the secret rocket works at Peenemünde, they would develop a deadly long-range rocket capable of carrying a one-ton warhead. Meanwhile, officials in the United States were showing not the slightest sign of interest in rocket research.

Goddard discovered this when, uncertain that the Guggenheim Foundation would renew his grant, he appealed to the government for funds to carry on his work. Once again, he offered his rockets to the United States government, pointing out their military applications—but both the army and navy turned him down. The army said it had no interest at all; the navy said it might be interested if and when Goddard "perfected" his rocket.

Meanwhile, Charles Lindbergh, always a staunch defender of Goddard's work, continued to urge the Daniel and Florence Guggenheim Foundation to renew its full support. Finally, in August 1934, Goddard received wonderful news—the foundation had voted to grant him new funds. He was to receive $18,000 for one year of research, with more to come if he made sufficient progress. One month later, Robert and Esther Goddard headed back to New Mexico in their red coupé. The crew, including Al Kisk, Charles Mansur, and Oley Ljungquist, a machinist who replaced Henry Sachs, followed.

Goddard was back where he wanted to be, in his "world of alkaline gray, holy, profane, grim, although exquisite with a haunting stillness." He dusted off the sweat-stained hat he had left behind on his workbench two years before, put on some old clothes, and drove out to Eden Valley to inspect the launch tower. He had left the tower intact, but in his absence everything that could be removed had been stripped away up to the 20-foot level. The steel shield, braces, cross pieces, ladders, and guy wires were all gone. Higher up in the tower, crows, using scraps of wire, had built nests so strong that wire cutters were needed to remove them. Still, within a few weeks, the ranch house and shop were restored to order, the boxes and crates of equipment were unpacked, the launch tower was repaired, and the rocket crew was ready for business.

Goddard was eager to get to work. Knowing that further support from the Guggenheim Foundation would depend on rapid progress, he planned to direct all his efforts toward achieving a high-altitude flight as soon as possible. A successful flight would prove that he was on the right track, and the sooner such a flight took place, the better. His thoughts were confirmed by Dr. Abbot of the Smithsonian, who wrote, "May I urge you to bend every effort to a directed high flight? That alone will convince those interested that this project is worth supporting. Let no sidelines, however promising, divert you from this indispensable aim which I hope you can accomplish with the grant you now have."

Soon after returning to Roswell, the Goddards received an unexpected visit from Charles Lindbergh and his wife, Anne. While taking Lindbergh on a tour of the shop and launch tower, Goddard carefully explained his plan to his distinguished visitor. First, he would improve the gyroscopic stabilizer; next, he would replace the nitrogen pressure tank with a small, lightweight pump; and when these had been successfully tested, he would work on reducing the weight of the rocket so that it could carry more fuel and thereby reach a greater altitude. Lindbergh, as always, was impressed with Goddard's logical, orderly approach, and he warmly reaffirmed his support and encouragement. He also urged the professor to think about publishing some of his results—but Goddard did not feel ready to do so.

The problem of how much longer he could keep his work secret was a source of great concern to Goddard. The stream of letters from abroad continued unabated, their writers asking for photographs, diagrams, and construction details. The letters came from Japan, Sweden, the Soviet Union, and many other countries. The most persistent requests, however, continued to come from Germany. Goddard was especially disturbed by statements that began to appear in German publications claiming credit for work that was clearly his own.

The situation at home was not much better. In the United States, the American Interplanetary Society (later renamed the American Rocket Society) had been founded in 1930 by a group of rocket enthusiasts. They had begun testing rockets that they said were "patterned . . . after one of the successful German liquid-fuel rockets." When Goddard reminded them that the first liquid-fuel rocket had been launched by him in 1926, the society's president, G. Edward Pendray, wrote to Goddard, insisting that he join its ranks, and adding, "your long silence is causing more harm to your reputation and to the development of rockets than any amount of idea-piracy that might occur as a result of greater frankness."

Goddard refused the invitation, preferring as always to work alone. "It happens," he explained in answer, "that so many of my ideas and suggestions have been copied abroad without the acknowledgment usual in scientific circles that I have been forced to take this attitude. Further, I do not think it desirable to publish results of the long series of experiments I have undertaken until I feel that I have made a significant further contribution to the problem."

Goddard knew that the pressure to release his findings would continue to mount, but he did not want to publish anything until he had something significant to report. Now that he was back again in New Mexico, he was determined to produce results. He did so quickly.

By the end of 1934, Goddard and his crew had built and tested a highly sophisticated, lightweight gyroscopic stabilizing system complete with tubes, pistons, valves, and vanes. They also worked on a parachute system that would prevent the rocket and its hand-tooled parts from crashing.

In January 1935, Goddard began a series of flight tests on his new gyroscopically controlled rockets. They varied in length from 13½ to 15 feet and weighed from 58 to 85 pounds without fuel and oxidizer. The first tests, made while the area was visited by the worst dust storms in its history, revealed flaws in the pressure system, the vanes, and the parachute release system.

For the next few weeks, Goddard worked to correct these problems. In a letter to Harry Guggenheim dated February 18, 1935, he was able to report, "the new control system, suitable for large light rockets as well as those we have used previously, has been further developed in field tests until it now launches the rocket in a thoroughly satisfactory manner. . . . We have had a streamline [sic] model of the rocket in flight, and have developed the parachute-releasing device so that it functions as soon as the rocket starts to descend."

Goddard's assistants placing one of his new "streamlined," gyroscopically controlled rockets in the launching tower, February 16, 1935.
(Goddard Collection/Clark University)

On March 8, 1935, he sent up another rocket. This one was equipped with an equalizer to prevent the liquid-oxygen tank pressure from exceeding the gasoline tank pressure; a pendulum stabilizer to substitute for the gyroscopic stabilizer, which was undergoing repair; and a 10-foot parachute. Within seven seconds, the rocket streaked to a height of 1,000 feet, then tilted to a horizontal flight, and crashed more than two miles from the tower. Even though the parachute had snapped off, Goddard was pleased. The rocket had traveled at more than 700 miles per hour—close to, or at, the speed of sound!

It was "the best flight we have ever had during the entire research," he wrote in a letter to President Atwood of Clark; "it looked more like a meteor passing across the sky than anything else." Goddard was making rapid progress—but there was so much more to do. "Father Time still has his foot way down on the accelerator," he wrote.

On March 28, Goddard was ready for another launch. This time, the rocket was fitted with a new, improved gyroscopic control that was set to apply controlling force when the axis of the rocket deviated 10 degrees or more from the vertical. At first, the rocket rose slowly from the tower. As Nell slowly gathered speed, Goddard could see that the gyroscopic control was working perfectly. It looked "like a long fish, swinging slightly back and forth each side of the vertical," he later wrote. Right on course, the rocket rose nearly a mile before its fuel was exhausted. Then it turned and streaked off into the distance, traveling nearly two and a half miles before falling to Earth. "It ought not to take many more flights, with a more rigid control vane system, before the flight can be kept vertical throughout," Goddard concluded.

If only the weather would cooperate. "Life here now is almost one continual dust storm," Goddard wrote in mid-April. He described one such storm this way: "It could be seen toward the east . . . as a long pale yellow cloud bank, with dark streaks rising up from the ground to the top, looking like scattered prairie fires. . . . When it struck, the wind was of gale force . . . and it was at times quite dark, with zero visibility."

On May 31, Goddard was again able to launch Nell (as Goddard affectionately named each new version of his rocket). This time, the rocket's gyroscopic control worked perfectly as it roared to a height of nearly a mile and a half. Another test, on July 12, was equally satisfactory.

Goddard was elated by the results, but he knew that flights of a mile and a half altitude were not the "high-altitude" flights his sponsors had hoped for. If he was ever to achieve flights of 30 or 40 miles above the Earth, he would have to develop a more powerful motor and build a much larger rocket. He envisioned more tests, with his rockets flying higher and faster than ever before. But his grant from the Guggenheim Foundation was about to expire. As he stood on the brink of success, Goddard was once again forced to ask for the two things he needed most—money and time.

CHAPTER 9 NOTES

p. 92   "Emerson says, 'If a man . . ." PRHG, Vol. II, p. 843.

p. 92   "Dark blue clouds in afternoon, . . ." PRHG, Vol. II, p. 765.

p. 94   "I think you are a good sport . . ." PRHG, Vol. II, p. 832.

p. 95   "You couldn't possibly stop him . . ." Milton Lehman, *This High Man*, p. 196.

p. 95   "Went to the cherry tree . . ." PRHG, Vol. II, p. 640.

p. 96   "All fame is relative, . . ." PRHG, Vol. II, pp. 843–45.

p. 96   "Perfectly amazing how things come to you, . . ." PRHG, Vol. II, p. 871.

p. 97   "world of alkaline gray, . . ." PRHG, Vol. II, p. 871.

p. 98   "May I urge you to bend . . ." PRHG, Vol. II, p. 888.

pp. 98–99 "patterned . . . after one of the successful . . ." Wernher von Braun and Frederick I. Ordway III, *History of Rocketry and Space Travel*, p. 78.

p. 99   "It happens that so many . . ." PRHG, Vol. II, p. 796.

p. 99   "the new control system, . . ." PRHG, Vol. II, p. 905.

p. 100   "the best flight we have . . ." PRHG, Vol. II, p. 908.

p. 101   "Father Time has his foot . . ." PRHG, Vol. II, p. 908.

p. 101   "like a long fish, . . ." PRHG, Vol. II, p. 910.

p. 101   "It ought not to take . . ." PRHG, Vol. II, p. 911.

p. 101   "Life here now is . . ." PRHG, Vol. II, p. 913.

10
WAR

"I still seem to be alone in my enthusiasm for liquid-fuel rockets, but I have a hunch that the time is coming when a good many will want to get aboard the bandwagon."
—Dr. Robert H. Goddard

Robert Goddard's years of struggle were yielding remarkable results, but he knew that others would have to be convinced if his work was to continue. Perhaps, if Harry Guggenheim were to see a rocket in actual flight, the foundation could be persuaded to support his research for another year. With this hope in mind, Goddard invited Guggenheim and Lindbergh to the Mescalero Ranch. In anticipation of their visit, he had his crew prepare two rockets for launching. In case something went wrong with the first rocket, the second would be there as a backup.

At sunrise on the morning after his guests arrived, Goddard drove them out to Eden Valley, where the latest version of Nell stood gleaming in the launch tower. Their faces glowed with expectation as Goddard started the ignition. A flame from the igniter licked at the nozzle, but nothing else happened. The rocket just sat in the launch frame. Goddard was embarrassed, but after examining Nell and calmly pointing out what had gone amiss, he asked his crew to bring out the replacement. Again, something went wrong; the backup rocket refused to rise. Goddard was mortified.

Despite the failures, Guggenheim and Lindbergh were impressed by what they had seen at the ranch. A few days later, Lindbergh wrote to Goddard, "I want you to know that I consider our visit with you very much worth while, even though we did not have the personal satisfaction of seeing a rocket in flight . . . [we] came back with the feeling that the project is being managed with unusual efficiency and intelligence, and that success is just a matter of time." In recalling the visit, Harry Guggenheim remarked that Goddard's faith in the ultimate success of his work was contagious. Best of all, the Guggenheim Foundation promptly renewed the grant for one more year.

While in Roswell, both Guggenheim and Lindbergh had made several suggestions. First, they urged Goddard to make a public announcement of the results of his work with liquid-fuel rockets. The last time he had informed the scientific community of his progress was in 1919; surely it was time to publish the results of his work with liquid-fuel rockets. Reluctantly, Goddard agreed.

The following year, on March 16, 1936, Goddard's report, titled *Liquid-Propellant Rocket Development*, was published by the Smithsonian Institution. In it, he briefly described his experiments since 1919, including his work with liquid oxygen and gasoline and his gyroscopic stabilizer, but omitting mention of his curtain cooling method and details of devices on which he was still working. The report did, however, establish that Goddard had flown the world's first liquid-fuel rocket in March 1926, a fact that had too often been overlooked or ignored both at home and abroad. It also proved that he had solved two of the three problems of rocket flight: first, he had solved the problem of providing a continuous flow of firing energy to the rocket with his invention of a combustion chamber, or rocket motor, that was extremely light and powerful and that could be used repeatedly; second, he had solved the problem of attaining stabilized directional flight with his invention of a highly sophisticated, automatic gyroscopic device no bigger than a large watch. The remaining problem, he concluded, would be to build a lighter rocket capable of carrying more fuel. Reducing the weight of the rocket by one-half would more than double the height to which such a rocket could be fired. His rocket had already traveled at more than 700 miles per hour, faster than the speed of sound—but to leave Earth entirely, it would have to go seven times faster.

Again at Lindbergh's urging, Goddard agreed to speak at a meeting of the American Association for the Advancement of Science. When he did so in December 1935, the scientific community began to take notice of his accomplishments. It was gratifying to have his work appreciated, but Goddard was interested neither in fame nor in wealth. He once wrote that

probably most research workers in pure science have no inspiration other than an intense interest in the work they are doing. If it happens that their achievements meet with very general public recognition, they are often more surprised and bewildered than elated. Their attitude of mind is, I believe, quite different from the outlook of those who struggle all their lives for the rewards most people think worthwhile.

Goddard nevertheless was always careful to put his name to his work. He kept thorough records to document his experiments and obtained patents on his major inventions. Yet when Lindbergh and Guggenheim suggested that he send one of his liquid-fuel rockets to the Smithsonian, where it could be made "a matter of record," Goddard protested. His rocket was not ready for public inspection, he said; it still needed development. Lindbergh patiently explained that the rocket need not be exhibited until Goddard gave his permission, but having it at the Smithsonian would prove, beyond question, the priority of his work.

At last, Goddard yielded and, in November 1935, Nell was greased and oiled inside and out, wrapped in old comforters, and carefully sealed in a coffin-like wooden crate. On arrival at the Smithsonian Institution in Washington, D.C., the crate was placed against a wall in a back room and a false wall was erected in front of it. There it would remain, hidden away from prying eyes, for many years to come.

The rocket buried away in the Smithsonian was the model that had attained an altitude of a mile and a half. To achieve flights of much higher altitudes, Goddard knew he would have to reduce the rocket's weight. He began working on a new, modified rocket that measured 13 feet in length and weighed about 200 pounds without fuel in its tanks—but tests with the rocket revealed a host of problems, especially with the curtain-cooling system. Sometimes, the rocket burned up in the launching tower; some-

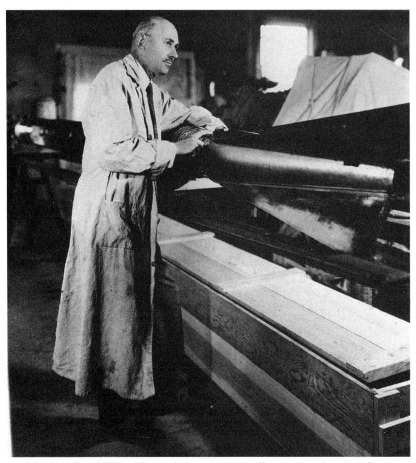

Goddard with "Nell" in his workshop at Roswell, New Mexico, October 1935. The wooden crate was used to ship this rocket to the Smithsonian Institution. (Goddard Collection/Clark University)

times it rose a few hundred feet before it fell in a shower of smoke and flame.

By 1937, Goddard was again at work redesigning the rocket. The new version of Nell was 16½ feet long and weighed only 100 pounds when empty. On March 26 of that year, Goddard tested the new rocket. "The rocket rose higher and more nearly vertical than in any previous flight," he wrote to Harry Guggenheim. "The other flights of the present series have been between 5000 and 7000 feet, but that of March 26 was between 8000 and 9000 feet. The height is somewhat uncertain as there was a slight haze in the air from a dust storm of the previous day, and the observer at the distant station lost sight of the rocket when propulsion ceased." It was his most successful flight. It did not achieve the high altitude he had

Flight of August 26, 1937—from a motion picture by Esther Goddard. A mechanically operated catapult was used to launch this rocket rapidly out of the tower. Rapid launching would be necessary for heavily loaded rockets. (Goddard Collection/Clark University)

hoped to reach but, at the time, it served to increase everyone's morale. Goddard was happy, and so was his crew. Best of all, the Guggenheim Foundation was encouraged to support Goddard's work for several more years.

His next task, Goddard decided, would be to design a fuel-feeding system that was less complicated and more dependable than the system he had been using. He suspected that the solution to the fuel-system problem would be found in one word: pumps. It occurred to him that a turbine (rotary) pump might prove to be the most efficient, so he set about designing a lightweight turbine pump unit capable of producing increased thrust.

As in earlier versions of Nell, liquid oxygen and gasoline were forced into the combustion chamber by nitrogen escaping from a pressure tank, although the nitrogen tank added undesirable weight to the rocket. Goddard decided to eliminate the tank and use in its place two small centrifugal pumps, one located between the gasoline tank and the chamber, and the other situated between the oxygen tank and the chamber. Next, he had to devise a control system so that the pumps, once started, would continue to operate throughout the duration of the flight.

The solution to starting the pumps and keeping them going was a turbine drive consisting of curved turbine blades mounted on a shaft inside the rocket. While the rocket sat in the launching frame, the turbine blades would be started by a flow of pressurized nitrogen. The nitrogen tank would not be attached to the rocket but would remain on the launch pad after the rocket took flight. Once set in motion, the turbine blades would revolve, along with the shaft to which they were attached, and this action would make the pumps work. To keep the turbine blades turning while the rocket was in flight, Goddard harnessed the power of some of the hot gases that ordinarily escaped through the rocket engine's nozzles. The gases would be forced through pipes where they would be converted into pressurized vapor; this vapor would keep the turbine blades revolving and they, in turn, would keep the pumps operating.

It was an ingenious idea, but one that took Goddard and his crew several years to develop. Centrifugal pumps existed, but they were too large and too heavy to be adapted for use in the rocket. "The development has now reached a crossroads," he wrote in a February 1938 report to the Guggenheim Foundation.

> *The work on high-pressure rockets, with more powerful chambers, may be continued. . . . On the other hand, I feel that there is no shortcut to high flights, and that work should be concentrated on pumps until a satisfactory pumping system has been made. . . . In view of the present state of world affairs it seems desirable to continue the work along the most advantageous lines, especially since the problem has been brought to a point where definite applications appear to be within reach.*

So, from 1938 to 1941, Goddard worked on making smaller and smaller turbine-driven pumps for liquid propellants. After much trial and error, he succeeded in making miniature pumps small enough to be held in the palm of one's hand yet powerful enough to drive rockets—"quarter-ton" rockets. In 1939, he began a series of tests using the tiny pumps in a 22-foot-long rocket that weighed from 190 to 240 pounds when empty. When fully loaded with liquid oxygen and gasoline, the rocket weighed nearly 500 pounds. At each step of the way, Goddard tried to make his rockets lighter in proportion to their size and, therefore, capable of carrying more fuel. The more fuel they carried, the higher they would be able to fly. As each problem was solved, the goal of high-altitude flight grew closer to attainment.

Day after day, Goddard was up before sunrise and out at the workshop or testing site. Every night found him hard at work trying to solve problems. There were many days when bad weather forced postponements of his tests, and there were days when nothing seemed to go right. Sometimes Nell rose only a few hundred feet before crashing in a burst of flame. Sometimes she didn't leave the launching frame at all. On one occasion, hoping to demonstrate a new pump rocket to Harry Guggenheim, Goddard had to chip ice from the rocket before launch, but the rocket never flew because ice had clogged the fuel lines. Ironically, except in Esther's motion pictures, Harry Guggenheim was never to see a Goddard rocket in flight.

Another disaster occurred in July 1938 when a tornado struck the launch tower, with the rocket in it, reducing everything to a mass of twisted wreckage. The crew was in tears, and Esther was sick with discouragement, but Goddard never faltered. He worked all day in the broiling heat to salvage whatever he could. The next day, Esther wrote,

> *I shall not forget how Bob looked. . . . Fatigue showed in every line of him especially his shoulders, bent forward, as they always are, to protect the weakness of his lungs. A man who 'should be in bed in Switzerland' coming in at 7:30 at night after a day that began at 3 in the morning. . . . And as he came in last night, almost staggering, the undefeatable was still in his eyes, and made me ashamed.*

Later that year, another storm touched Goddard with its fury. It formed off the coast of Africa, roared across the Atlantic, and tore up the east coast of the United States, leaving havoc and destruction in its wake. When it reached New England, the hurricane swept over Worcester and Goddard's house on Maple Hill, where it ripped out several trees, including an old, gnarled cherry tree in the backyard. Goddard learned of the catastrophe in a letter from his tenants. "Cherry tree down," he wrote in his diary. "Have to carry on alone."

As he worked toward perfecting his rockets, Goddard developed nearly all of the basic components that are now used in rockets and guided missiles, including gyroscopic controls, curtain-cooled combustion chambers, pump-and-turbine assemblies, automatic ignition and releasing systems, clustered engines, gimbal-mounted tail sections, and many others. Some of his ideas, such as using solar energy to operate rocket motors in space, existed only on paper but were later developed by others.

By the late 1930s, Goddard knew that his days as a solitary rocket scientist were coming to an end. Both at home and abroad, younger men were following in his pioneering footsteps, and the time was fast approaching when further rocket development would require large teams of scientists and engineers. Already, Harry Guggenheim and Charles Lindbergh were urging him to consider outside help. The Guggenheim Foundation would not be able to afford the time and cost of such one-man development forever. Years later, government engineers who spent in one week what Goddard spent in a lifetime would be awed by what the Yankee professor had been able to accomplish. But at the time, Goddard sensed that his dream was coming to an end, and he silently wondered what role he would play in the new age that was fast approaching.

But Goddard's dream, like the dreams of many other people, was interrupted by events across the Atlantic. On September 1, 1939, Nazi Germany invaded Poland, and the continent of Europe erupted in war. In the course of a few months, Hitler's Panzer tanks would sweep over one country after another, and the Luftwaffe would prepare to bomb England into submission. After the Japanese attack on Pearl Harbor on December 7, 1941, the United States would be drawn into the conflict as well.

Goddard immediately offered his assistance to the military. Once again, the army failed to recognize the potential importance of Goddard's rockets. The navy, however, accepted the professor's offer and, in 1941, he began to do research for the military. The following year, the navy asked him to move to Annapolis, Maryland, to assume the role of director of research on jet propulsion at the navy's Bureau of Aeronautics. In July 1942, the Goddards closed up the ranch house and workshop in Roswell "for the duration," expecting to be gone for only a few months. When he returned, Goddard planned to continue his high-altitude rocket research. But that hope was destined to remain unfulfilled; it was the last time that he would ever see Roswell.

Goddard sent this picture of his February 1940 pump-turbine type rocket to Harry F. Guggenheim in December 1944, after German V-2s began falling on London. On the back, he wrote, "Rocket produced in New Mexico . . . It is practically identical with the German V-2 rocket." The rocket is now in the National Air and Space Museum of the Smithsonian Institution, Washington, D.C. (Goddard Collection/Clark University)

At Annapolis, Goddard's first assignment was to develop liquid-fuel rocket motors that would help heavily loaded bombers and seaplanes take off from short runways and provide the power needed for fast climbs. This system was the same jet-assisted takeoff, or JATO, system Goddard had once before proposed to the military—the system that they had then rejected. Fortunately, Goddard had been able to bring his crew with him to Annapolis. Thoroughly versed in the operation of JATO, Goddard and his crew quickly perfected the system and successfully flight-tested it many times.

Another assignment was to develop a variable-thrust rocket motor that could be controlled by a pilot. The motor had to be extremely powerful but designed in such a way that the pilot could speed it up or slow it down quickly. It was an extremely challenging project—a small malfunction of the fuel system could result in an explosion—but after many months of hard labor, Goddard produced a rocket airplane motor that functioned perfectly. In a few seconds, it could be accelerated from idling speed to the speed necessary for takeoff. In the air, a pilot could make the plane do anything he wanted. Years later, high-altitude supersonic aircraft, including the X-1 and the X-15, were fitted with engines based on Goddard's design. It was in such a plane that Chuck Yeager became the first pilot to break the sound barrier.

Goddard's last project for the navy was to adapt a small pressure-fed liquid-fuel rocket for use as a guided missile. After more than 30 years of high-altitude rocket research, the work seemed rather dull. He was anxious to return to New Mexico, to Nell, and to the work he loved.

Despite the boredom he felt, Goddard, as always, gave his best—but in 1943, the long, exhausting hours of work began to catch up with him. The first signs of trouble were a series of persistent "colds" that left him with a constant cough. Suspecting that his old tuberculosis problem had returned, Goddard reluctantly submitted to an examination. His doctor advised him that there was no cause for alarm and recommended that he give his throat a rest by not talking. But as the weeks and months passed, Goddard's voice began to fail noticeably. Esther tried to convince him to give up his contract with the navy and return to Roswell, but he insisted that his "laryngitis" would pass.

Robert H. Goddard, June 1945. (Goddard Collection/Clark University)

But the old intensity and determination seemed to have deserted him. In March 1945, in a letter to a friend, he wrote, "By 6:30 P.M. I am ready to flop into an easy chair by the fireplace with a 100 watt lamp and what I hope will be a good book." A few days later, he entered in his diary a quote from a book he was reading: " 'From nerve and muscle strained already almost beyond endurance he squeezed somehow the last half-ounce of effort that means success . . . ' "

When Goddard returned for another examination in May, his doctor discovered a small growth in the professor's throat and sent him to see a throat surgeon in Baltimore. On June 19, 1945, he underwent an operation to remove the growth. Upon examination, the growth was found to be cancerous, so a second operation was scheduled for the purpose of removing more tissue.

Goddard could no longer speak, so he communicated by writing notes to those around him. Each day he asked to see the newspapers. On August 6, when Goddard read the headlines announcing that the United States had dropped a new kind of bomb on Hiroshima, he held up his hand and made the "V" sign for victory. On August 9, he read that a second nuclear bomb had been dropped on Nagasaki. The following day, at nine o'clock in the morning, Robert Hutchings Goddard quietly passed away.

On August 14, 1945, while the nation was celebrating the surrender of the Japanese, Goddard was buried near his parents in Hope Cemetery, not far from Maple Hill, in Worcester, Massachusetts.

CHAPTER 10 NOTES

p. 103	"I still seem to be alone . . ." PRHG, Vol. III, p. 1386.
pp. 103–104	"I want you to know . . ." PRHG, Vol. II, pp. 940–41.
p. 105	"probably most research workers . . ." PRHG, Vol. II, p. 730.
p. 105	"a matter of record, . . ." PRHG, Vol. II, p. 937.
p. 106	"The rocket rose higher . . ." PRHG, Vol. II, pp. 1054–55.
pp. 108–109	"The development has now reached . . ." PRHG, Vol. III, p. 1127.
p. 110	"I shall not forget . . ." Milton Lehman, *This High Man*, p. 252.
p. 110	"Cherry tree down . . ." PRHG, Vol. III, p. 1216.
p. 113	"By 6:30 P.M. I am ready . . ." PRHG, Vol. III, p. 1579.
p. 114	" 'From nerve and muscle . . .' " PRHG, Vol. III, p. 1583.

11

EPILOGUE

"I feel we are going to enter an era comparable in its progress to that in which the airplane advanced. . . . It's just a matter of imagination how far we go with rockets and jet planes. . . . I think it's fair to say you haven't seen anything yet."
—Dr. Robert H. Goddard

Shortly after her husband's death, Esther Goddard sold the Mescalero Ranch, which the Goddards had finally purchased some years before. Before turning it over to the new owners, she retrieved two pump-model rockets and a miscellaneous collection of valves, fuel tanks, and motors from the dusty workshop. She left what remained of the old launch tower out at Eden Valley. Poachers had already stripped away everything usable, and the desert winds and sands had begun their ceaseless task of burying all traces of her husband's rocket firings. It seemed that in the unsettled postwar world, Robert Goddard's name would be forgotten as well. When the nation focused on New Mexico, it saw only Los Alamos, where a team of physicists had developed the atomic bomb, and Trinity, the site of the world's first nuclear explosion.

When Americans heard the word *rockets*, they thought of the deadly V-2 rockets that the Germans had launched against England. No one seemed to remember that the bazooka rocket—the weapon American foot soldiers had used to stop German tanks—had been invented in 1918 by a reclusive American scientist. Confirming the popular belief that rockets and space flight were German inventions was the fact that, shortly after the war, 118 German rocket scientists were brought from the Nazi rocket works at Peenemünde to the United States to develop missiles for the army. Among those who came were Hermann Oberth, Walter Dornberger, and the flamboyant, outspoken Dr. Wernher von Braun.

Within a short time, von Braun and his team demonstrated their "superiority" by successfully launching high-altitude missiles at the Redstone Arsenal in Huntsville, Alabama. No one called von Braun a crackpot when he urged the government to accelerate rocket technology in order to compete with the Soviet Union, America's new adversary. And no one called him a "mad scientist" when he spoke dramatically of interplanetary flights, of space probes, of men on the moon. America listened—and acted. The nation's annual budget for rocket development and manufacture rose quickly to more than $1 billion. The space race was on.

Hardly anyone noticed when, in 1947, workmen at the Smithsonian Institution quietly removed the false brick wall behind which Goddard's 1935 rocket was hidden. Without fanfare, the rocket was uncrated and put on display. Nell, still well-polished and well-oiled, had her own place of honor. Close by was Lindbergh's plane, *The Spirit of St. Louis.*

In that same year, Esther Goddard began the arduous task of sorting and organizing her husband's papers and notes. Among them, she found drawings and descriptions for an astonishing number of devices that he had never patented. With the approval of Harry Guggenheim, and with the help of Charles Hawley, Goddard's patent attorney, Esther filed claims for the devices in her husband's name. During the next 10 years, 131 patents were issued posthumously to Goddard.

Meanwhile, rockets had developed into a multi-billion-dollar industry. But hardly a rocket went aloft that did not infringe on Goddard's patents. In 1951, Esther Goddard and the Guggenheim Foundation brought suit against the government for infringements of Goddard's work. Nine years passed before the suit was finally settled with an award of $1,000,000. In making the award, the new National Aeronautics and Space Administration (NASA) announced, "Dr. Robert H. Goddard's work as a universally recognized pioneer in rocketry has recently formed the basis of a settlement . . . of $1,000,000 for rights to use over 200 of Dr.

Robert H. Goddard in his laboratory at the Mescalero Ranch near Roswell, New Mexico, 1935. (Goddard Collection/Clark University)

Goddard's patents which cover basic inventions in the field of rockets, guided missiles, and space exploration." As its share of the award, the Guggenheim Foundation received back more than it had granted to Goddard during his lifetime. More important, however, the suit established beyond question the precedence of Goddard's work.

Gradually, Goddard's achievements gained recognition. The old launch tower, repaired and repainted, was installed in the museum in Roswell along with other rocket memorabilia. In September 1959, the U.S. Congress voted to honor Goddard posthumously with the Congressional Gold Medal, the country's highest decora-

This postage stamp, issued in 1964 to honor Robert H. Goddard, shows an Atlas rocket and the launching tower at Cape Kennedy (now Cape Canaveral). (U.S. Post Office)

tion for civilians, "in recognition of [his] pioneering research in rocket propulsion." In June 1960, the Smithsonian Institution, which had supported Goddard's research for so many years, awarded him the rare, gold Langley Medal for "achievements in aerodromics," an honor bestowed on only eight men before him. The following month saw the unveiling of a granite marker, presented by the American Rocket Society, on the site of his 1926 launching at Aunt Effie's farm in Auburn, Massachusetts.

On March 16, 1961, exactly 35 years after Goddard's pioneer flight of a liquid-fuel rocket, NASA dedicated its brand-new space facility in Greenbelt, Maryland, to Goddard's memory. The Goddard Space Flight Center was NASA's first major scientific laboratory devoted entirely to the exploration of space.

More honors followed in quick succession. Students at the Air Force Academy compete for the Goddard Award for achievement in mathematics. Robert Hutchings Goddard professorships honor scientists who teach at Princeton University and the California Institute of Technology. On July 2, 1962, the U.S. House of Representatives passed a bill establishing March 16 as a day of national tribute to Goddard. And on Goddard's birthday, October 5, in 1964, the U.S. Postal Service issued a stamp in commemoration of his work.

Had Goddard been alive to accept the honors, he probably would have quickly tired of all the fuss. Throughout his lifetime, he was both a solitary genius and a dauntless researcher who sought results rather than recognition. With calm optimism, he translated the fantastic into theory and the theoretical into reality. Today, the operation of every space vehicle is based upon his ideas, his inventions, and his careful research.

In the decades following Goddard's death, astronautics has grown into a highly respected science. The space race, accelerated by the launching of Sputnik in 1957, captured the imagination of all humankind. In a few short years, the world saw humans walk on the moon. Later, it witnessed men and women working in space shuttles and space stations and saw space probes chart the outer

The space shuttle on the launching pad at night. (NASA)

reaches of the solar system. Today, plans are being laid to colonize the moon and to send astronauts to Mars by the year 2016. To accomplish these goals, space scientists say they will need nuclear-powered rockets capable of lifting much heavier loads than rockets now in use. These new rockets would use a nuclear reactor to heat the propellant, which in turn would be expanded by a supersonic nozzle to produce thrust. Of course, the idea really isn't new; it is only one of many still-untested ideas buried away in Goddard's notebooks.

Robert Goddard would have enjoyed hearing President George Bush when he recently told a group of students, "You are coming of age during a golden age of space. . . . It's time to open up the final frontier. There can be no turning back." When a reporter later asked how the United States could get to Mars, the president answered, "You have to go fairly fast. It's a long way out there."

No one knew better than Robert Hutchings Goddard how far the journey was, or how fast one had to travel. His were the first footsteps in the human quest for unknown worlds. His memory soars with every rocket; his spirit mingles with the stars.

CHAPTER 11 NOTES

p. 115   "I feel we are going . . ." PRHG, Vol. III, p. 725.
pp. 116–117   "Dr. Robert H. Goddard's work as . . ." PRHG, Vol. III, p. 1596.

MILESTONES IN THE ROCKET EXPERIMENTS OF ROBERT H. GODDARD

Dr. Robert Hutchings Goddard, pioneer physicist and engineer, laid the technical foundations for today's long-range rockets, missiles, Earth satellites, and space flight. In the course of establishing and demonstrating the fundamental principles of rocket propulsion, he founded a whole new field of science and engineering. Here, briefly, are a few of Goddard's historic achievements. He was the *first* to:

- explore mathematically the practicality of using rocket power to reach high altitudes and shoot to the moon (1912)
- receive a U.S. patent on the idea of multistage rockets (1914)
- prove, by actual experiment, that a rocket will provide thrust in a vacuum—that it does not need air to push against (1915)
- develop and demonstrate the basic idea of the bazooka (1918)
- publish in the U.S. a basic mathematical theory underlying rocket flight and propulsion (1919)
- develop a rocket motor using liquid propellants (liquid oxygen and gasoline) (1920–25)
- develop and launch a liquid-fuel rocket (March 16, 1926)
- launch a scientific payload (camera and barometer) in a rocket flight (1929)
- use deflector vanes in the rocket motor blast as a method of stabilizing and guiding rockets (1932)

- develop gyroscopic stabilization and control apparatus for rocket flight (1932)
- launch a liquid-fuel rocket that traveled faster than Mach 1, the speed of sound (1935)
- launch a rocket with a motor pivoted in gimbals controlled by a gyroscopic mechanism (1937)

Dr. Goddard was also the first to develop pumps suitable for rocket fuels, self-cooling rocket motors, variable-thrust rocket motors, and practical rocket-landing devices. The basic designs for such launch vehicles as the Atlas, Thor, Jupiter, and Redstone rockets were worked out by Dr. Goddard before 1940.

Goddard received 83 patents on his rocket and space ideas during his lifetime. After his death, his executors found among his research notes and diaries ideas that resulted in 131 additional patents.

GLOSSARY

black powder: an explosive mixture of potassium nitrate, charcoal, and sulfur. A variety of gunpowder, it is used in ammunition for guns and in blasting.

cellulose nitrate: a substance formed by the action of nitric acid on some form of cellulose such as paper, cotton, or linen. It is used to make explosives.

gyroscope: a device consisting of a heavy metal disk mounted on a spindle (or axis) around which it rotates freely. The spindle is in turn confined in a framework that is also free to rotate around one axis or two. Gyroscopes have two qualities that make them useful. First, the axis of a free gyroscope will remain fixed in one position unless external forces act upon it, much the way the axis of a spinning top remains upright unless something interferes with its motion. Second, a gyroscope can be made to deliver a torque that is proportional to the angular velocity about a perpendicular axis. Both qualities stem from a principle called "conservation of angular momentum." According to this principle, in any system of particles, the total angular momentum of the system relative to any point fixed in space remains constant, provided no external forces act on the system. Because of their unique properties, gyroscopes are used to provide fixed reference directions for compasses on ships and aircraft. They are also used in space vehicle stabilization systems.

hydrogen: the simplest and lightest of the elements, it is normally an odorless, colorless, highly flammable gas. When it is cooled to -423 degrees Fahrenheit, hydrogen becomes a liquid. Liquid hydrogen, commonly used to fuel rocket engines such as those on the Space Shuttle, is the second coldest liquid on Earth.

When liquid hydrogen is burned with liquid oxygen (lox), the temperature in the shuttle engine's combustion chamber reaches more than 6,000 degrees Fahrenheit, higher than the boiling point of iron. Because it uses liquid hydrogen and liquid oxygen as fuel, the shuttle's engine—although it is not much larger than an automobile engine—generates 100 horsepower for each pound of its weight, while an automobile engine generates one-half horsepower for each pound of its weight.

jet: the forceful stream of gases discharged through the nozzle of a jet engine. A jet engine produces forward propulsion by discharging a jet of gases through one or more exhaust nozzles. Jet airplane engines use surrounding air for the combustion of fuel; rocket engines carry both fuel and all oxygen needed for combustion.

nitrocellulose smokeless powder: *See* cellulose nitrate and smokeless powder

nitroglycerine: an oily, extremely dangerous, poisonous, explosive liquid used in making dynamite.

payload: the load carried by a spacecraft that consists of things or passengers related directly to the purpose of the flight, as opposed to things such as fuel that are needed for its operation.

propellant: a mixture containing both fuel and an oxidizer.

rocket engine: unlike ordinary engines, a rocket engine contains or carries along with itself everything it needs to operate, including the substances it needs for the combustion of its fuel. Because it does not require intake of outside substances, it is capable of operating in outer space.

rocket fuel: the ideal rocket fuel is relatively light in weight and burns at very high temperatures. A variety of substances or combinations of substances are now used as rocket fuel.

smokeless powder: also called nitrocellulose smokeless powder. An explosive consisting of cellulose nitrate suspended in a gelatinlike substance; it produces very little smoke when it explodes.

speed of sound: the speed of sound varies depending upon the medium through which it passes. For instance, sound travels faster in water than in air, and even faster in iron and wood.

Generally, the speed of sound (Mach I) is placed at 1,088 feet per second at sea level at 32° F. When a rocket or plane breaks the sound barrier (i.e., flies faster than sound travels), listeners on the ground hear "thunderclaps," but people aboard these craft do not hear them.

theodolite: an optical instrument that consists of a sighting telescope mounted on a stand so that it is free to turn in any direction. Theodolites are used by surveyors to calculate vertical and horizontal angles and to measure distances.

thrust: the pushing or pulling force generated by a rocket engine.

torque: a force that causes rotation or torsion. In an automobile, the engine delivers torque to the drive shaft, making it spin; the rotating drive shaft in turn sets the wheels in motion, making the automobile move.

turbine: a rotary engine that has a series of curved blades or vanes attached to a central rotating spindle. The engine is set in motion when a pressurized current of fluid (such as water or steam) is directed at the vanes.

FURTHER READING

BOOKS BY ROBERT H. GODDARD

Liquid-Propellant Rocket Development. Washington, D.C.: Smithsonian Institution, 1936. Goddard's account of his experiments with liquid-fuel rockets through 1935.

A Method of Reaching Extreme Altitudes. Washington, D.C.: Smithsonian Institution, 1919. Goddard's basic mathematical theory underlying rocket propulsion and rocket flight, now considered a classic document of astronautics.

Rockets. New York: American Rocket Society, 1946. Contains facsimiles of the two Smithsonian reports, with a new foreword by Goddard.

Rocket Development: Liquid-Fuel Rocket Research 1929–1941. Edited by Esther C. Goddard and G. Edward Pendray. Englewood Cliffs, N.J.: Prentice-Hall, 1948. Goddard's detailed account of the experiments he conducted at Roswell, New Mexico, during the 1930s.

The Papers of Robert H. Goddard. 3 volumes. Edited by Esther C. Goddard and G. Edward Pendray. New York: McGraw-Hill, 1970. This massive collection contains Goddard's autobiography; extensive notes on his experiments; excerpts from his diaries; letters he wrote and received; newspaper accounts; the texts of his reports to the Smithsonian, Clark University, and the Guggenheim Foundation; and much, much more. Although difficult to find, these volumes offer a firsthand, intimate look at Goddard and his work.

BOOKS ABOUT ROBERT H. GODDARD

Deutherty, Charles. *Robert Goddard: Trail Blazer to the Stars.* New York: Macmillan, 1964. A lively biography for young readers.

Lehman, Milton. *This High Man.* New York: Farrar, Straus and Company, 1963. A full-length, definitive biography of Goddard.

Richards, Norman. *Dreamers and Doers: Inventors Who Changed the World.* New York: Atheneum, 1984. Contains a concise biography of Goddard.

Verral, Charles S. *Robert Goddard: Father of the Space Age.* Englewood Cliffs, N.J.: Prentice-Hall, 1963. This popular children's book introduces young readers to Goddard's life and work.

SCIENCE FICTION BOOKS THAT INFLUENCED GODDARD

Serviss, Garrett P. *Edison's Conquest of Mars.* Los Angeles: Carcos House, 1947.

————. *A Columbus of Space.* New York: D. Appleton & Co., 1911.

Verne, Jules. *From the Earth to the Moon, All Around the Moon: Space Novels.* Translated by Edward Roth. New York: Dover Publications, Inc., 1962.

Wells, H. G. *Seven Science Fiction Novels.* New York: Dover Publications, Inc., 1962. Contains *The First Men in the Moon, The War of the Worlds, In the Days of the Comet*, plus four other full-length novels.

BOOKS ABOUT ROCKETRY AND SPACE TRAVEL

Hundreds of excellent books dealing with rocketry, spacecraft, and space travel are available in libraries everywhere. The books listed here are well-established "classics" written for ordinary readers.

Asimov, Isaac. *The Intelligent Man's Guide to Science.* Vol. I. New York: Basic Books, 1960.

Clarke, Arthur C. *The Exploration of Space.* New York: Harper & Brothers, 1951.

Emme, Eugene M. *History of Rocket Technology.* Detroit: Wayne State University Press, 1964.

Ley, Willy. *Beyond the Solar System.* New York: Viking Press, 1964.

————. *Rockets, Missiles and Space Travel.* New York: Viking Press, 1954.

Logsdon, John. *Decision to Go to the Moon.* Cambridge: MIT Press, 1970.

von Braun, Wernher, and Frederick I. Ordway III. *History of Rocketry and Space Travel.* New York: Thomas Y. Crowell Company, 1966.

Winter, Frank H. *Rockets Into Space.* Cambridge, Mass., and London: Harvard University Press, 1990.

Wolfe, Tom. *The Right Stuff.* New York: Farrar, Straus & Giroux, Inc., 1979.

BOOKS BY CHARLES A. LINDBERGH

These books contain references to Lindbergh's relationship with Goddard and to Lindbergh's ideas about space flight.

Of Flight and Life. New York: Charles Scribner's Sons, 1948.

The Spirit of St. Louis. New York: Charles Scribner's Sons, 1954.

The Wartime Journals of Charles A. Lindbergh. New York: Harcourt, Brace, Jovanovich, Inc., 1970.

INDEX
Numbers in italics refer to illustrations

A

Abbot, Dr. Charles G., 41, 68, 74, 77–78, 79, 83, 95
Across the Zodiac (book), 6
Adams, Dr. W. S., 78
aerodynamics, 34
aeronautics, 78, 82, 111
Aldrin Jr., Edwin E., 2
American Association for the Advancement of Science, 27, 105
American Interplanetary Society—*See American Rocket Society*
American Rocket Society, 98–99
Andrews, Calvin H., 13
aneroid barometer, 70
"Anniversary Day," 13, 17, 26, 48, 86
"Apparatus for Igniting Liquid Fuel" (patent), 96
Armstrong, Neil A., 2
Army Signal Corps, United States, 36
atomic energy, 21
Atterlay, Joseph, 6
automobiles, 31

B

Babcock, Dr. Harold D., 78
balloons, 7–8
   Newton's third law, 24
bazooka, *37*, 51, 115, 121
Bell, Alexander Graham, 46
Bliss, Charles H., 14
Bliss, Robert, 14
Boston American (newspaper), 42
Boston Globe (newspaper), 72

Boston Herald (newspaper), 42
Boston Post (newspaper), 6
Breckinridge, Henry, 94–95
Brick Moon, The (book), 6
Brooks, Dr. Charles F., 84

C

Camp Devens (Massachusetts), 74, 79, 83
Carnegie Institution (Washington, D.C.), 77, 78
centrifugal force, 13
Clark University (Worcester, Massachusetts), 25–26, 27, 31, 52–53
clustered engines, 110
combustion chamber, 29, 51, 63, 69, 86–89, 104, 108, 110
"Concerning Further Developments of Rocket Method of Investigating Space" (report), 43
curtain cooling method, 69, 88, 96, 104, 105, 110

D

Daniel Guggenheim Fund for the Promotion of Aeronautics, 82
Daybreak (poem), 83
deflector vanes, 121
Die Rakete zu den Planetenräumen (The Rocket into Planetary Space) (book), 45
displacement-current experiments, 28
Dornberger, Walter, 97, 116
double-acting engine, *57*
du Pont, Henry, 77

E

Eden Valley (New Mexico), 86, 95, 97, 103
Edison, Thomas Alva, 3
Edison's Conquest of Mars (story), 7
electricity, 4, 16, 27
electron theory, 27
Esnault-Pelterie, Robert, 45
exhaust nozzles, 29, 33, 34, 51, 87

F

"Father of Modern Rocketry," 44
frogs, 4–5
From the Earth to the Moon (book), 6
fuel-feeding system, 108–109

G

gimbal-mounted tail sections, 110
Goddard, Esther, 55–56, 58, 64, 67–68, 84–85, 86
Goddard, Fannie Hoyt, 3–4, 10, 47
Goddard, Nahum Danford, 3–4, 9, 14, 56, 69
Goddard, Robert Hutchings, *2, 5, 37, 40, 54, 57, 66, 90, 93, 106, 113, 117*
  "Anniversary Day," 11–13, 17, 26, 48, 86
  childhood, 3–6
  Clark University
    student career, 25–26
    teaching career, 27, 31, 33–34
  death of, 114
  early education, 9–10, 13–15
  frog studies, 3–5
  funding
    Guggenheim grant, 79–80, 82–83, 94
    Lindbergh aid, 76–80, 97
    Smithsonian grant, 35–36, 53, 95
  health problems, 10, 28–29
  Lindbergh visit, 75–77
  media coverage, 39, 41–44
  Mescalero Ranch, 84–85, 85–91, *93*, 97
  "Method of Reaching Extreme Altitudes," 35, 41, 45
  milestones, 121–122
  Mount Wilson Observatory, 36
  Newton's third law, 24–25
  Oberth and, 45–46
  patents, 27, 29, 96, 122
  postage stamp, *118*
  Princeton University, 27–28, 31
  rocket development
    balloon experiments, 7–8
    combustion chamber, 29, 51, 63, 69, 86–87, 88–89, 104, 108, 110
    curtain cooling method, 69, 88, 96, 104–105, 110
    exhaust nozzles, 29, 33–34, 51, 87
    first theories, 9
    fuel-feeding system, 108–109
    gyroscopes, 15, 17–18, 20, 86, 88–90, *90*, 95–96, 98–101, 104, 122
    ignition systems, 69
    liquid-fuel rockets, 39, 51–52, 53–55, *62, 66*, 104, 112
    lox, 54–55
    multi-stage rockets, 16, 29–30, *30*
    notebooks, 27
    propulsion systems, 17, 21–22, 28–29
    solid-fuel rockets, 36, 50–51
    vacuum tests, 33–34
  space travel
    science fiction, 6–7
    theories on, 16, 21, 31, 41–44
  test flights, 31–32, 60–73, 87–91, 98–101, 103–105, 106–107
    first flight, 61–68, *66*
    launching sites, 69, 85–86
    test ban, 71–73

weapons research, 36–37, 46,
52, 111–114
bazooka, 37
wedding, 56
Worcester Polytechnic Institute, 18–20
World War II, 111–114
Goddard Space Flight Center
(Greenbelt, Maryland), 118
gravity, 7–8, 33
Greg, Percy, 6
Guggenheim, Daniel, 82, 88
Guggenheim, Harry, 82, 99, 103–104, 106, 109, 110, 116
Guggenheim Foundation, 79–80,
97, 109, 110, 116–117
guided missiles, 112
gyroscopes, *90, 100*
automatic device, 104
essay on, 20
stabilization system, 86, 88–90,
95–96, 98–101, 104, 110, 122
theories on, 15, 17–18

H

Hale, Edward Everett, 6
Hawley, Charles, 116
Herschel, Sir John, 6
high-altitude rockets, 78, 111
High Speed Bet, The (short story),
20
Hitler, Adolf, 96
hydrogen—*See also liquid hydrogen*
balloon experiments, 7–8
rocket propulsion, 25

I

Icaro-Menippus (book), 1
ignition systems, *64, 65,* 96, 110
Industrial Revolution, 1
ion propulsion, 22, 27, 43

J

JATO (jet-assisted takeoff), 112

jet propulsion, 111

K

Kisk, Albert, 70, 83, 97
Kisk, Esther—*See Goddard, Esther*
kites, 4, 15

L

"Last Migration, The" (paper), 47
Ley, Willy, 46
light waves, 27
Lindbergh, Anne, 98
Lindbergh, Charles A., *80,* 94
Goddard aid, 76–80, 82–84, 97,
103–104
Goddard visit, 75–77, 98–99
liquid-fuel rockets, 51–52, 53, *62,
66*
first rocket, 62–63, 98–99, 121
flight testing, 60–73
public report, 104
weapons research, 112
liquid hydrogen, 25, 43–44, 52
liquid oxygen (lox), 25, 43–44,
52, 54–55, 58, 61, 63, 65, 88, 108
liquid oxygen tank, *65*
Liquid-Propellant Rocket Development (report), 104
liquid propellants—*See liquid hydrogen; liquid oxygen*
Little Nell, 87, 101, 103, 105, *106,*
116
Ljungquist, Oley, 97
lox (liquid oxygen)—*See liquid oxygen*
Lucian of Samosata, 1
Lunar Discoveries (story), 6

M

magnetism, 27
Mansur, Charles, 83, 97
Mansur, Lawrence, 70, 83
Mars (planet), 6, 11
Martin, Dr. C. F., 78

Maxim, Hiram S., 3
"Mechanism for Directing Flight" (patent), 96
Merriam, Dr. John C., 77, 79
Mescalero Ranch (Roswell, New Mexico), 85–91, 92–94, 97–101, 103
metallurgy, 34
"Method and Means for Producing Electrically Charged Particles" (patent), 27
"Method of Reaching Extreme Altitudes, A" (paper), 35, 41, 45
Michelson, A. A., 25
microscope, 4
moon, the
  Goddard's theories, 33
  landing on, 2–3
  literature on, 6
  media coverage, 41–44
Mount Wilson Observatory (Pasadena, California), 36, 78
multi-stage rockets, 30
  moon landing, 76
  patent on, 121
  theory of, 25, 29–30, 41
  Tsiolkovsky writings, 44–45
  weather forecasting, 53

N

NASA (National Aeronautics and Space Administration), 43, 116, 118
National Aeronautics and Space Administration—See NASA
"Navigation of Interplanetary Space, The" (paper), 31
"Navigation of Space, The" (article), 16
Navy Bureau of Aeronautics, United States, 111
Navy Bureau of Ordinance, United States, 52
Newton, Sir Isaac, 24
Newton's Third Law, 24, 33

New York Times, The (newspaper), 42
nitrous oxide, 52
nozzles—See exhaust nozzles

O

Oberth, Hermann, 45, 116
Olmstead, Miriam, 14
"On Some Peculiarities of Electrical Conductivity Exhibited by Powders and a Few Solid Substances" (papers), 26
"On the Possibility of Navigating Interplanetary Space" (paper), 21
oxygen, 63—See also liquid oxygen
  balloon experiments, 7
  rocket propulsion, 25

P

parachute system, 86, 88, 99
patents, 27, 29, 96, 122
Peenemünde Rocket Works (Germany), 97, 116
Pendray, G. Edward, 99
Pioneer 10 (spacecraft), 43
Poe, Edgar Allan, 6
Popular Astronomy (magazine), 21
Popular Science News (magazine), 15, 16
Princeton University (New Jersey), 27–28, 31
propulsion systems
  liquid-fuel rockets, 25, 39
  theory of, 17, 21, 28–29
  Tsiolkovsky writings, 44

R

rocket motor, 64
rocketry
  centrifugal force, 13
  combustion chamber, 29, 51, 63, 69, 86–87, 88–89, 104, 108, 110

curtain cooling method, 69, 88, 96, 104, 105, 110
exhaust nozzles, 29, 33, 34, 51, 87
fuel-feeding system, 108–109
gyroscopes, 15, 17–18, 20, 86, 88–90, 95–96, 98–101, 104, 122
ignition systems, *64*, 69
launching systems, 58, 69
liquid-fuel rockets, 51–52, 53, *65*, 112
"Method of Reaching Extreme Altitudes," 41
milestones, 121–122
multi-stage rockets, 25, 29–30, 53
Newton's third law, 24–25
Oberth research, 45–46
parachute system, 86, 88, 99
propulsion theories, 25–38, 28–29
rocket motor, *64*
rocket tests, 31–32
solid-fuel rockets, 36, 53
space travel theories, 41–44
test flights, 60–73, 87–91, 98–101, 106–107, *107*
    first flight, 61–68, *66*, 121
    test ban, 71–73
Tsiolkovsky writings, 44–45
vacuum tests, 33–34
V-2 rocket, 46, 96, 111, 115
weapons research, 36–37, 46, 52, 111–115
weather forecasting, 46, 53
Roope, Percy, 64, 66, 70
Roosevelt, Theodore, 15
Rutherford, Ernest, 25

S

Sachs, Henry, 61, 64, 66, 70, 83, 97
Sanford, Edmund C., 55
Scientific American (magazine), 4, 15, 20, 21
Serviss, Garrett P., 6–7, 11
Smithsonian Institution (Washington, D.C.), 35–36, 41, 43, 53, 60, 104, 105, 116

smokeless powder, 32, 36, 50
solar energy, 22, 110
solid-fuel rockets, 50, 53
sound barrier, 112
Sousa, John Philip, 15
space shuttle, *119*
space travel
    Goddard theories, 16, 21, 31, 41–44
    literature on, 1, 6
    moon landing, 2
    multi-stage rockets, 30
step rockets—*See multistage rockets*
stratosphere, 33

T

telegraphy, 16
telescope, 4, 21
thermodynamics, 34
thermometer, 70
"Traveling in 1950" (article), 19
Tsiolkovsky, Konstantin Eduardovitch, 44–45
tuberculosis, 28–29, 85

U

"Use of the Gyroscope in the Balancing and Steering of Airplanes, The" (essay), 20

V

vacuum tests, 33–34, *40*, 121
Vera Historia (book), 1
Verne, Jules, 6, 7, 11, 16
Volterra, Vito, 26
von Braun, Wernher, 46, 97, 116
Voyage to the Moon, A (book), 6
V-2 rocket, 46, 96, 111, 115

W

Ward, Effie, 61, 64
Ward Farm (Auburn, Massachusetts), 61, 69–70, 72

War of the Worlds (book), 6
Washington Star (newspaper), 39
Weather Bureau, United States,
  46, 53, 78
weather forecasting, 53
Webster, Dr. Arthur G., 26, 41
Wells, H. G., 6, 11, 90
White, Oscar, 85–86
Wilson, Woodrow, 28
Wolcott, Dr. Charles D., 35
Wood, Robert Williams, 26
Worcester Evening Gazette (news-
  paper), 39
Worcester Evening Post (newspa-
  per), 72

Worcester Polytechnic Institute
  (Massachusetts), 18–20
Worcester Telegram (newspaper),
  56
World War II (1939-45), 111–114

X

X-1 (aircraft), 112
X-15 (aircraft), 112

Y

Yeager, Chuck, 112
Young, Jim, 8